During his long and distinguished career in film and broadcasting, Dennis Marks made several documentaries on cultural subjects ranging from Janáček to Russian history. During the 1990s, he was General Director of English National Opera. His search for Joseph Roth grew out of his acclaimed BBC Radio 3 series on the Habsburg Empire, *Faultline*. He died in 2015.

Dennis Marks

—

WANDERING JEW

—

The Search for Joseph Roth

 Notting Hill Editions

Published in 2011
by Notting Hill Editions Ltd
Widworthy Barton, Honiton, Devon EX14 9JS
This edition published in 2017

Designed by FLOK Design, Berlin, Germany
Typeset by CB editions, London

Printed and bound
by Memminger MedienCentrum, Memmingen, Germany

A CIP record for this book
is available from the British Library

ISBN 978-1-910749-71-5

www.nottinghilleditions.com

Contents

The search for Joseph Roth

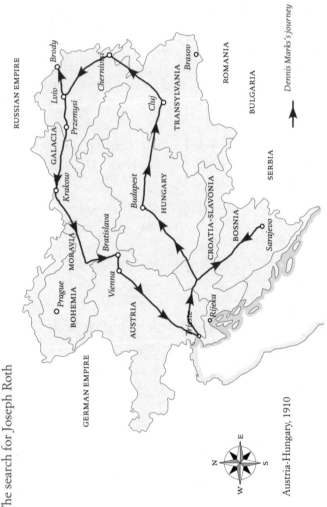

Austria-Hungary, 1910

—► Dennis Marks's journey

— WANDERING JEW —

One

– 'A Man Seeks His Fatherland' –

He keeps disappearing. Ten years ago I thought that I had found him, on the wrong side of the tracks in the little town of Brody, on the dusty eastern edge of Europe, where the Empire of the Habsburgs once dissolved into the Empire of the Romanovs. I had come to Brody at the end of a fitful eight-week journey along the boundaries of that Empire, across Austria to the fringes of Italy, down into former Yugoslavia and through Hungary and Romania to the muddy marches of Western Ukraine. I was keeping a bargain I had made with myself thirty years earlier.

I first encountered *The Radetzky March*, one of the masterpieces of modern German fiction, while I was researching a BBC film about Vienna at the turn of the twentieth century. Its opening paragraphs promised a stirring narrative of the end of empire. Then for the next 300 pages it systematically broke that promise. I was led to expect weighty historical events distilled into the tale of a single imperial family. Instead I was taken on a wild goose chase from one provincial garrison to another in the company of officers who had nothing better to do than drink, gamble, get into debt and beguile the time with desultory affairs. Between its opening in 1859 and its final pages set six decades later almost nothing happened. There were two sexual encounters, a duel and an industrial strike, but they were all left unresolved. Even the Great War and the death of the longest surviving European monarch were brushed aside with casual disregard. It was the least epic historical novel I had ever read and I was totally seduced by it. I was captivated by its glimpses of a vanished world seen through the wrong end of a telescope and framed in dreamlike prose which kept slipping out of reach. It was elusive and ironic and it stuck like a burr in my brain.

I knew little of Habsburg history and even less of the author. I soon discovered that I was not alone. Even today there is no English biography of Joseph Roth and only a couple of academic studies, one of which is currently remaindered. His personal life is cloaked in mist. Yet the landscape he described was unforgettable and I was impatient to encounter it at first hand. I swore that one day I would follow the novel's sad and confused hero Carl Joseph von Trotta along the margins of Mitteleuropa. I would drink in faded cafés across the road from crumbling opera houses. I would buy second-class tickets in Kaiser-yellow railway stations and take rickety trains from Slovenia and Moravia in the west to the dank marshes of Galicia in the east.

It was fifteen years before I could keep my promise to myself. Three decades ago the borders of Europe and Russia were still in Neville Chamberlain's words 'a faraway country of which we know little'. Then in the late 1980s the landscape of Poland, Czechoslovakia and Ukraine was radically transformed. The Iron Curtain lifted to reveal one perfectly preserved stage set after another, all painted in faded pastels – the pink, green and gold favoured by Emperor Franz Joseph. Beyond the urban scenery of Mitteleuropa sat the smudged landscape of muddy plains, framed by dense wooded hills, familiar to me from the journeys taken by Carl Joseph during the novel. Much of it had scarcely changed since he crossed it with his mistress in a *wagon lit* just before the First World War. As I followed the railway tracks eastward through towns with evocatively unpronounceable names like Brno, Cluj and Przemysl, I could see how fifty years of communist paralysis had frozen the frame. Across the Great Hungarian Plain and through the forests of Trans-Carpathia, where farmers wearing embroidered smocks drove ox carts loaded with logs along tracks crowded with geese, I seemed to be watching a 1930s movie played in reverse. Surely now I could match Roth's misty hypnotic descriptions of Galicia with the reality which inspired them. Perhaps, when I reached his birthplace, I might even be able to construct a psycho-geography of the author –

what German speakers call his *seelenlandschaft*, his spiritual landscape. But when I arrived in his homeland another promise was broken. The scenery was intact but the screenwriter had left the set.

It might have helped if I had known that I was being led through the swamps by one of literature's most prodigious liars. Joseph Roth, born in 1894 in what is now Western Ukraine and buried in the Paris suburbs a mere forty-five years later, the victim of drink and despair, lived a life as clouded and obscure as his remarkable fiction. In his diaries and letters, in his reported conversations and his confessional journalism, he scattered falsehoods like a Ruthenian peasant sowing corn. As a novelist, he constantly blurs historical truth and hallucination. As a reporter, his documentary accounts of the years after the Great War are bent out of true by his wounded subjectivity. At first glance, his sidelong descriptions of the end of three European empires seem almost cinematic. That is another illusion. If there is anything filmic about Roth's work, it is its debt to the expressionist German movies which he reviewed in the smoky Berlin picture houses of the 1920s. Like the films of Murnau and Pabst and the paintings of Grosz and Dix and Beckmann, his stories belong in the world of *Die Neue Sachlichkeit* – the 'new objectivity' which was the house style of Weimar Germany. That term is also misleading. Grosz's drawings are no more objective than Roth's writing. In his published work, every phrase, each observation bears witness to the fragility of fact. His accounts of his own life are even more flimsy. Nothing stands up to close examination. His biographer David Bronsen calls him a mythomaniac. The Ukrainian scholar Larisa Cybenko prefers the term 'fantasist'. The English literary critic Jon Hughes argues that even his narrative voice is a fabrication. In several of his stories he introduces a character with the name Joseph Roth who simultaneously acts in the drama and observes it from the edge of frame. I soon learned that the writer I had chosen as a tour guide through Eastern Europe after the fall of the Berlin Wall was a compulsive falsifier.

Consider the bald facts of his life. He was born a hundred and twenty years ago on the borders of Austria and Russia. He studied in Lemberg and Vienna and enlisted in the imperial army during the Great War. He worked as a journalist in Berlin during the Weimar Republic, in post-revolutionary Russia and in Paris when it was Europe's creative fulcrum. Yet the further he travelled from his birthplace, the more his fiction returned to the eastern provinces of Franz Joseph's former empire. The little Jewish town where he spent the first eighteen years of his life appears under one fictitious name or another in nine of his fifteen novels. It is peopled with deserting soldiers, Hasidic Jews, dealers in drink and contraband, human traffickers, revolutionaries, prostitutes, and all the other flotsam which drifted across Western Ukraine during and after the Great War. Most of his characters are compulsive shape-changers. Their identities are as diffuse and slippery as the surrounding marshes. Even the solid Habsburg cities where some of them settle have a history of constant flux. Between the two world wars, the regional capital of Galicia changed its name and nationality four times. When Roth was born, it was Austrian Lemberg. In 1918, during the short-lived Ukrainian Republic it was called Lviv. After the Treaty of Saint Germain it was incorporated into Poland under its old name of Lwow. When the Russians invaded in 1941 it was submerged in the Soviet Socialist Republic of Ukraine as Lvov. Almost all the eastern Habsburg cities changed their names. Tarnopol became Ternopil and Czernovitz was first Cernauti then briefly Chernovtsy, briefly Cernauti and finally Chernivtsi once again as it passed from Austria to Romania to Poland to the Soviet Union. Today these bi-polar towns are all in the Republic of Ukraine and that word contains the secret of their fluid identity. In Russian and in Ruthenian – the nineteenth-century term for the local Slavic vernacular – *U kraina* means 'at the border'. It is neither in one place nor another. Ukraine is one of the most displaced places in Europe and Joseph Roth was its unreliable laureate.

When you survey the fragments of autobiography he scattered throughout his writing and conversation you can see his mythomania in action. He told his friends and colleagues that he was born in Schwabendorf, a German colony in Volhynia. When at the end of his life he toyed with conversion to Catholicism, he persuaded a priest to furnish a baptism certificate which named his birthplace as Schwaby. He claimed to be Austrian on his father's side and Russian on his mother's side. He manufactured a dozen different identities for his father. In one version he was the son of a celebrated Viennese armament maker known as 'Le Cartouche Rouge'. In another he was the illegitimate offspring of a high Austrian civil servant. Sometimes he claimed that his mother's husband was not his father and that he was of noble descent – 'the natural son of a Polish Count'. Alternatively he was the son of a painter or an officer with a girl in every garrison. He often signed himself 'Joseph Roth former lieutenant in the 24th Lancers of the imperial royal army'. He insisted that when Franz Joseph was buried, he had been part of the military escort. He spoke of being captured and transported to the eastern front in the Great War and of serving time as a prisoner of war in Siberia. He said that for his military achievements he had been decorated with the silver medal of the order of Charles I. Not one of these statements is true.

To begin at the beginning (which Roth rarely does), he falsified his birthplace. Schwabendorf, which means 'Swabian settlement', does not exist.

There may have been Swabian colonies in these borderlands but they were almost certainly not in Volhynia. If you consult a map of Eastern Europe in the early 1900s, you will see that Volyn is the old name for the northern half of Galicia where Russian was spoken and not Ukrainian. Roth's homeland was firmly in the Ruthenian southern part of the province. I know this to my cost. When I first visited Galicia I wasted an entire day in search of Schwabendorf. I asked the eager young travel agent who was organising my journey to help me locate the town and we pottered around the Lviv *oblast* trying to find it. It was a trip back in time as well as in space. We saw low vernacular cottages and decrepit inns which had been untouched for fifty years. In a particularly muddy tangle of villages we were becalmed in our car for forty minutes by a slow-moving herd of cattle and an ill-tempered flock of geese. However, we found no trace of Schwaby or Schwabendorf. After searching for hours in the gathering dusk for a petrol station to fill our almost empty tank, we returned to my hotel none the wiser. It was only then that I discovered we had driven a hundred and fifty kilometres in the wrong direction.

After dinner I fell into conversation with an English couple at the next table. They told me that the previous day they had travelled to Brody to visit the house of their Polish grandfather. En route they had passed the Rudolf Gymnasium, where he was educated, and noticed a rather primitive sculpture on the grass outside commemorating four celebrated alumni. One of these local heroes was Joseph Roth. He was identified not as a novelist or journalist but as a 'famous anti-fascist'. Armed with this information and reassured that something had survived from Roth's youth we set off the following day in the correct direction. This time we were much more successful in our search. A room inside the Gymnasium was set aside as a miniature Joseph Roth museum. There were faded photographs, copies of his work in German and a couple of Ukrainian translations. Unfortunately that was all. There were no memorabilia, no documents and nothing to guide us to his birthplace. Municipal and synagogue records had perished during the Second World War when Brody was pulverised by invading armies from east and west. The charming nineteenth-century buildings pictured in yellowing photographs were gone and in their place were rain-streaked concrete flat blocks. There was scarcely a house surviving from the 1930s, let alone from four decades earlier. As for Schwabendorf, no one had ever heard of it.

Someone suggested that Roth might have been referring to a district to the south of the railway tracks called Schwaby. So we mooched around the streets behind the station looking for hints. It was no easy task. The old Kaiser-yellow station, second cousin to every terminus from Zagreb to Oradea, had been blown up by the Russians when they drove out the Nazis in 1945 and the Soviets had replaced it with a functional red-brick box.

I had almost given up the search when I stumbled across the one street in town which carried the writer's name – Vulitsa Josefa Rotha. It was only a few metres from the railway sidings and it petered out into the dust and scrub on the edge of the rusty tracks. This was a little more encouraging. If this desultory no-man's-land was his real birthplace then it might offer an explanation for all the contradictions and false trails which crowded his life. Perhaps he was ashamed of being born on the wrong side of the tracks. It would interlock neatly with his invention of a fantasy father and a genealogy of Polish counts and Austrian arms manufacturers. I clung to this hypothesis for several years and even incorporated it into a BBC radio series I made about the Habsburg borderlands. At one point I drew the inevitable comparison between Roth and Gustav Mahler, the son of a Jewish publican who grew up in the equally nondescript provincial Moravian town of Jihlava. It was a seductive comparison. There are indeed superficial similarities between the Galician author and the Moravian composer. They each incorporate traces of their early experience into their art. The barracks and the dance hall are rarely absent from Mahler's symphonies and they provide a backdrop to many of Roth's stories. However, the resemblance ends there. While Mahler commanded the heights of Austrian cultural life, Roth retreated to its margins. A visit to Vienna's House of Literature confirmed that Vulitsa Josefa Rotha was yet another blind alley. Heinz Lünzer, Austria's principal living Roth scholar, showed me maps of Brody in the 1890s. He pointed out a crossroads with a few scribbled notes beside it. Most scholars now agree that Roth grew up not in Schwaby, let alone the fictitious Schwabendorf, but in an unidentified and long-abandoned rooming house on the main road leading north from the central marketplace. It was clear that I had little hope of finding Roth's origins by searching in the railway sidings or tramping through the muddy borderlands.

I had even less faith in what survived in the archives. Roth systematically obscured almost every aspect of his early life, beginning with his name. Before he left Brody to study in Lemberg, every document refers to him as *Moses* Joseph Roth. However in 1916, when he enlisted at the age of twenty-two to serve in the Kaiser's army, he suppressed his first name. Moses vanished and its place was taken by Joseph. His fakery did not end there. When he was with friends and family, he replaced Joseph with his childhood diminutive of 'Mu', explaining that Mu was short for Muniu, which he claimed was a diminutive of the name Solomon. Then to complicate matters still further, he enlarged Muniu into '*Muniu faktisch'*. According to his biographer David Bronsen, he acquired this pseudonym as a child because he was in the habit of adding the word *faktisch*, which is the German for 'in fact' or 'really', to his fanciful table talk. This gives us a vivid picture of an imaginative child spinning stories in adult company. It does not explain why he obliterated Moses and persisted with *faktisch* into adult life. Of course Jews have regularly altered their names. In 1939 my own father changed his surname from Yarsakovitch to Marks in response to army clerks who had difficulty pronouncing foreign words. In Roth's extended collection of essays about the life of Eastern Jews, published under the title *The Wandering Jews*, he devotes several paragraphs to the subject of unstable Jewish names. In a characteristic tongue-in-cheek passage he explains how for the authorities they were nothing but trouble:

All Christians have sensible, European names. Jewish names are mad and Jewish. Nor is that all. They have two or three surnames . . . You never know what to call them.

However, there is nothing mad or even complicated about the name Moses. If, as some scholars have suggested, Roth was in denial about his Jewish origins it seems rather eccentric to replace an Old Testament prophet with a biblical king. When he added the word *'faktisch'* to *'Muniu',* it was almost as if he was challenging his hearers to contradict him just as he did at his mother's dinner table. His later distortions are even more difficult to understand. When he married a pretty young Galician girl in Vienna in 1922, why did he fake his mother's name on the marriage certificate? His wife Friedl was also of Jewish stock and they married in a synagogue, so it cannot have been simply to hide his origins. Why did he remove his debut novel *The Spider's Web* from his published list of works and later insist that his first work of fiction was *Hotel Savoy*? Was it to dissociate himself from its fascist central character when fascism was on the rise in Austria? It is hard to believe that the Austrian censors would have been fooled for a second. Or was it simply that for Roth, falsehood was always more interesting than reality?

When we scrape the surface of these untruths we can just detect the reality behind them. Roth's friend Soma Morgenstern published a collection of reminiscences on the centenary of Roth's birth which casts revealing shafts of light on his later years. One intriguing memory relates to his final days in Paris. He tells us that in the late 1930s the novelist regularly burned the midnight oil with a Lithuanian friend Joseph Gottfarstein and in their late-night conversations Roth offered up an alternative version of his origins. By then his memory was blurred with drink and depression but it has the ring of truth to it. The Austrian officer, the arms manufacturer and the Viennese painter of his imagination are replaced by Nochum Roth, a failed businessman with a loveless marriage and a fragile grasp of reality who abandoned his son at the age of eighteen months. Nochum had ambitions to be a prosperous timber merchant and hop trader but he was no more successful as an entrepreneur than as a husband. The final chapter of this tale is rather confused but it appears that he had some kind of nervous breakdown during a trip to Hamburg. After failing to close a business deal, he set off back to Galicia. His behaviour in the railway carriage became increasingly bizarre and aggressive and in Berlin he was forcibly removed from the train. His fellow passengers arranged for him to be admitted temporarily to a Prussian mental hospital whose director managed to contact his in-laws. They moved him to the house of a Hasidic rabbi with a reputation as a miracle healer. According to Gottfarstein, Nochum died insane in the rabbi's home.

Through this story we can glimpse a possible psychological explanation of Roth's mythomania. He had every reason to conceal his father's mental illness. He may well have feared that his father's paranoia was clinical and possibly hereditary. This is speculation of course. We are on firmer ground when we consider the social motive for his fabrications. In the 1880s, when his parents married, Brody was a prosperous town, crowded with Jewish visitors from every corner of the Empire. It attracted migrants for two reasons. To begin with, it was a major junction on the direct route between Russia and Poland. In 1773, the Emperor Joseph II visited Brody and elevated it to a Habsburg *freistadt*. As it was less than twelve kilometres from the Russian border and on two major trade routes – east/west from Kiev to Warsaw and Vienna and north/south down to Odessa and Istanbul – it was ideally placed to be a free port. The Kaiser confirmed the town's new status in 1779 and for almost a century anything exported and imported through Brody was free of customs duty. Over the next century the little *stetl* grew into a substantial town and it became a magnet for eastern Jews. We should remember that until 1867 Jews were forbidden to join guilds or reside in Vienna. However, in free towns like Brody they could trade and raise capital to support commerce and manufacture. By the 1880s the number of Jews in the town had risen to 20,000 – more than 65 per cent of the population. Because of its commercial significance it became known as the Trieste of the east.

Apart from its prosperity, Brody also had a spiritual reputation. For many years, it had been an important centre of Hebraic learning, which earned it the title of 'the Polish Jerusalem'. Among those drawn to the town were growing numbers of Hasidic Jews, followers of the mystic rabbi Baal Shem Tov, who had settled there in the late eighteenth century.

Hasidim, with their characteristic long black gabardine coats and florid side-locks, make a regular appearance in many of Roth's novels. In his collection of essays *The Wandering Jews*, he includes a moving section describing the celebration of the Jewish Day of Atonement in Galicia, and in *The Radetzky March* there is a crucial encounter between Franz Joseph and the Hasidim of the border *stetl* where Carl Joseph is stationed. The followers of Baal Shem Tov were conspicuous not only for their striking dress but also for their noisy and exhibitionist public displays of faith. The indigenous Christian population – Russian Orthodox, Polish Catholics and Ukrainian Uniats – were very hostile to the Hasidim, not only because of their histrionic behaviour but also because they envied their economic success. Brody became something of an anti-Semitic joke and its ultra-Orthodox population were soon known as the *narunim* or fools of Brody. This would have been enough to embarrass Roth when he looked hungrily towards cosmopolitan Vienna. Then in 1883 Brody suffered further misfortune. Its *freistadt* status was withdrawn. Its economy collapsed and it ceased to be an important crossroads. The railway line was redirected and Brody began the slow decline from Jerusalem into a ghost town.

Without a father and with an impoverished fatherland, it is hardly surprising that Roth should have been restless and eager to leave his birthplace.

He also had an ambitious, protective and control-ling mother. Like so many provincial Jews in the Empire, she surely knew that her son's future would be more secure away from the underprivileged east. For Habsburg provincials, particularly Jews, suc-cess meant reaching the imperial capital. Austria-Hungary may have been the multi-ethnic home to more than twelve nationalities but at heart the Empire was centripetal. Vienna was a magnet for Czechs, Hungarians, South Slavs and Ruthenians.

This was particularly true for Galicians in the years after Roth matriculated from the Rudolf Gym-nasium. Although the Ruthenes were among the Em-peror's most loyal subjects, this loyalty was bought at a price. The local gentry were predominantly Polish and the regional capital Lemberg was a particularly Polish town. Its architecture, its customs and its cul-ture all looked back to the years before the Polish partitions when it was part of the great Lithuanian-Polish commonwealth. Franz Joseph wished to maintain multicultural equilibrium in Galicia and recognise its indigenous languages and traditions. So when the teaching medium in schools was sud-denly switched from German to Polish, Roth found himself becalmed in a Polish/Ruthenian/Jewish backwater. He was not the first writer to wish to draw a double line under his provincial past.

After secondary school, he passed quickly through Lemberg University and then continued his graduate studies in the grand neoclassical pile on Vienna's Ringstrasse. In the accounts of his Viennese contemporaries and the few surviving photographs, we can see a rather inhibited lower-middle-class provincial *stetl* boy transforming himself into a literary dandy. His tastes in clothes, food and drink, not to mention politics and literature, show him comprehensively airbrushing out his Galician past. Indeed, between his arrival in Vienna in 1913 and his death twenty-six years later he returned to Ruthenia only three times on very brief visits.

Yet his writing tells a totally different tale. From his very beginnings as an author, first in Vienna and then in Berlin and Paris, his fiction and his journalism were constantly drawn back to his homeland. Galicia makes its first appearance in his second novel, *Hotel Savoy*, published in 1924. This takes place in a border town described as 'the gateway to the West'. Critics have often assumed that it is Lodz because of an incident in the novel describing the violent suppression of industrial action. Roth encouraged this when he later confessed to stealing the story of the strike from a fellow writer. However, Lodz was never a border town, and apart from the presence of industry everything else in the book smells and tastes of Lemberg. In the opening chapters of the novel, the hero Gabriel Dan describes his impressions of the town during his first evening on the western side of the Russian border. When I first visited Lviv I decided to stay in the distressed elegance of the Hotel Zhorzh, which made up in historical resonance what it lacked in hot water and reliable electricity. Unable to shower or shave, I strolled round the corner to the central market square. Every scent and sound – the cries of headscarfed babushkas, the pickled cabbage and the honey in the comb – echoed Roth's description of a Galician regional capital:

It must have been market day. Hay and chaff were scattered about the pavements, shops were just being shut, locks were clicking, chains were rattling, householders were making for home with little handcarts, women wearing bright head-scarves were hurrying, carefully carrying full pots in front of them and bursting market bags over their arms with wooden spoons sticking out of the top. A few lanterns cast their silvery light into the dusk, the pavements turned into a parade where men in uniform and civilian clothes twirled their slender canes and waves of Russian scent ebbed and flowed.

Similar border towns recur constantly in his fiction. His next novel, *Flight Without End*, begins in the fictitious Galician town of Shmerinka, just over the Russian side of the border. In *The Wandering Jews*, written between these two novels, Roth devotes a long chapter to a description of a typical *stetl* on the Russian/Polish border where Jews were compelled to live during the empire of the Romanov tsars:

The little town lies in the middle of a great plain, not bounded by any hill or forest or river. It runs out into the plain. It begins with little huts and ends with them. After a while the huts are replaced by houses. Streets begin. One runs from north to south, the other from east to west. Where they intersect is the marketplace. At the far end of the north-south street is the railway station.

A similar small Jewish town in the Pale of Settlement is the setting for his first commercially successful full-length work, *Job: The Story of a Simple Man*, where it goes by the name of Zuchnow. The garrison town in *The Radetzky March* is never named but its central marketplace, railway station and hotel are first cousins to those in Brody. The nearby fictional village of Burdlaki is placed only a few miles from the Russian frontier.

Throughout the 1930s almost every work has Galician links and Roth no longer tries to conceal them. *Weights and Measures* takes place in a hamlet which is actually called Schwaby. The novel's preoccupation with contraband and commercial crime suggests exactly the kind of *freistadt* Roth inhabited during his childhood:

Leibusch Jadlowker owned the border tavern and no one knew how it came into his possession . . . Ne'er do wells and criminals frequented Jadlowker's frontier tavern; he harboured vagrants, beggars, thieves and robbers and his cunning was such that the law could not touch him. His papers and those of his guests were always in order. The official informers, who swarmed near the frontier like flies, could report nothing detrimental, nothing immoral, about his way of life.

In *Tarabas* we are in Koropta, described as Russian but to all intents and purposes Ruthenian. Brody itself makes a brief appearance in *The Bust of the Emperor,* like Alfred Hitchcock creeping into the corner of frame in one of his films. The small town of Lopatyny where it takes place is described as being off the railway line between Brody and Przemysl. Although much of *The Capuchin Crypt* (also published in English translation under the title *The Emperor's Tomb*) occurs in Vienna, Slovenia, Baden and even Siberia, it constantly returns to Zlotogrod, the invented Galician town that regularly stands in for Brody in his later work. Just to reinforce the biographical link, the name 'Zlotogrod', which means 'golden town' in both Russian and Polish, echoes the name of Brody's main thoroughfare which today is still called Golden Street. His birthplace even haunts Roth's writing after his death. His posthumously published novella *Leviathan* tells the story of a coral trader in a Galician *stetl*. All these Brody lookalikes share the same landmarks: a central crossroads with a market square, a tavern managed by a Jew, a hotel with a café where the officers drink and a station buffet where they lunch. At one end of town is a barracks and at the other is a cemetery. On the edge are marshes where frogs croak and mosquitoes bite and in the distance is a low curtain of hills.

This raises an obvious question about Roth's ambivalent relationship with Galicia. If he was compelled to conceal and distort his own past, why does his writing constantly revisit it? In his absorbing study *Understanding Joseph Roth* Sidney Rosenfeld has no doubt that the answer is autobiographical. He argues that Roth's entire life and work are a spiritual quest for a lost father and fatherland. He reminds us that *The Capuchin Crypt*, the sequel to *The Radetzky March* which takes the story of the Trotta family up to the eve of the *Anschluss*, was originally entitled 'A Man Seeks his Fatherland'. At the very end of the novel, its central character – Carl Joseph Trotta's cousin – is left adrift in Vienna without a home or a purpose in life. His final words – 'So where could I go now, I, a Trotta' – echo Roth's own sense of displacement. Rosenfeld concludes that the melancholy which permeates all his fiction and much of his journalism is the product not only of the loss of his homeland but also the betrayal of his Jewish identity after he abandoned his Galician comfort zone.

This is a tempting path to follow but it is a dangerous one. It risks confining his work to a box marked 'Habsburg Jewish nostalgia'. However, his characters tell a different story. They are as self-contradictory as their creator. His imperial functionaries are locked in a dysfunctional empire and his *stetl* Jews are often canny and unprincipled survivors. Carl Joseph's father, a provincial Habsburg bureaucrat, has his tender and touching moments but for the most part he is a remote anachronism, personifying the self-destructive rigidity of Austria-Hungary's final years. The Jewish human-trafficker Kapturak is clever and resourceful but he is also quick to exploit and if necessary betray his fellow Jews. Roth knew from his youth that victims could also be predators. His fictionalised Galicia is a tapestry in which the positive and negative strands of the dying monarchy are interwoven.

Roth's own statehood was as complex and ambiguous as the home territory of his fiction. He is usually described as an 'Austrian' writer but this is an over-simplification. It is true that he was born and died an Austrian. However, when his Austro-Hungarian homeland was dismembered in 1918 and Galicia was annexed by Poland after the Treaty of Versailles, Roth found himself with an unwanted Polish passport. His response was instant. He quixotically applied for Austrian citizenship. He then perversely abandoned Vienna and spent his twenties and early thirties as an itinerant scribbler in Berlin, Paris, Russia, Albania and the south of France. At no point in his post-war adult life did he really inhabit the country which today we call Austria. He was the archetypal displaced person and an Austrian in name only. In 1933 when Hitler rose to power he went into permanent exile. His very restlessness makes him impossible to pin down. His writing is as fluid as his nationality. His language is German, but his subject matter is often Slavic, sometimes Jewish and always extra-territorial. It is this sense of perpetual motion both in his prose and his subject matter which characterises his vision of the world rather than the subconscious guilt at betraying his Jewish origins diagnosed by Rosenfeld. In his displaced sensibility he is a true son of the borderland. Wherever he sets his narrative – in Germany, Austria, France or Russia – he speaks in the accents of Galicia. His love of paradox and contradiction, which makes his novels so haunting, is buried deep in his homeland's history and geography

Galicia certainly had more than its fair share of both. In its Habsburg high season at the beginning of the twentieth century it stretched from the Polish border west of Przemysl to Tarnopol on the frontier with Tsarist Russia, up to Sandomir in the north and down to the border with Romanian Bukovina. In its marketplaces and trading inns Polish, Russian, Romanian, Ukrainian, German and Yiddish were all spoken by the local population. These languages took root during half a millennium of occupation by neighbouring kingdoms and empires. The most prominent historian of Western Ukraine, Jaroslav Hrytsak, has unearthed early records which explain its complex demography. The first references to Galicia describe it as a region of White Croatia. Then at the end of the tenth century it became the easternmost extension of Moravia. In the twelfth century it sat on the frontier between Ukrainians and Poles. By the turn of the fourteenth century it was controlled by Hungarians – hence the Habsburgs' claim to the territory. It crossed religious and cultural frontiers as well as political ones. In its early days, it was the point where the Mongol invasion halted. After the Mongols retreated it was the dividing line between Roman and Orthodox Christianity. For the next four centuries, during the rule of Polish kings and Habsburg emperors, it remained a region of restless displacement. Even after the Treaty of Versailles it continued to be tossed backwards and forwards between Russia, Ukraine and Poland before it was finally incorporated into the enlarged Polish nation state. It was everywhere and nowhere, the archetypical borderland.

Hrytsak goes even further; he argues that Galicia never really existed. Before the 1800s, no one described themselves as a Galitzianer. The region was a Habsburg construct; it was invented at the end of the eighteenth century to confront Russian Orthodoxy with Austrian Enlightenment. The Habsburg monarchy intended it to be a kind of eastern Switzerland, ethnically and religiously mixed but culturally enlightened, with German as its lingua franca. This offers another explanation of Roth's ambivalent relationship with his homeland. In his imagination he remodelled Austria-Hungary into a kind of anti-nation-state – a composite of everything that was uprooted by the Treaty of Versailles – and a sanctuary for all the orphaned peoples scattered in the wake of the Great War. It was defined by being both multicultural and extra-territorial. Roth's most eloquent expression of this alternative reality is in his late novella *The Bust of the Emperor*. Its central character is Count Morstin, the former governor of a Galician province. He is so traumatised by the Kaiser's death that he invents an elaborate daily ceremony in which he salutes a rough vernacular stone image of the deceased Franz Joseph. When the local Polish gentry mock and criticise him he arranges a formal burial for the Emperor's bust and delivers a passionate threnody for the dead Empire:

I hate nationalism and nation states. My old home the Monarchy alone was a great mansion with many doors and many chambers, for every condition of men. This mansion has been divided, split up, splintered. I have nothing more to seek for there. I am used to living in a home, not in cabins.

This passage is sometimes dismissed as a symptom of Roth's retreat into alcohol-induced nostalgia. However, read in the context of Hrytsak's thesis it is powerfully symbolic. Count Morstin's panegyric is a plea for a tolerant future to preserve the multicultural past. By extension Roth's fictional borderlands can be seen as a vision of an alternative homeland for displaced persons everywhere.

The same principle underpins Roth's own flexible identity and that of his characters. Shape-changing is a strategy for survival in a world where borders have always been blurred and nation states have regularly died one evening only to be reborn as somewhere different the next morning. In order to survive, the displaced need multiple identities. Roth once admitted to friends that 'I lived several different existences.' This reveals more than just a penchant for invention and elaboration. It is a declaration of kinship with all the displaced people who surrounded him in his youth and accompanied him throughout his years of exile. Roth fabricates from political necessity as much as personal loss. If we wish to find *Muniu faktisch*, he is sitting in a Paris café or a Berlin *kneipe* observing his fellow exiles and turning them into literature. He knows that he is an unreliable narrator. When he inserts a fictitious Joseph Roth into *Flight Without End,* he is glorying in his own unreliability. He is *Muniu* nicht *faktisch*.

As D. H. Lawrence once remarked, 'Never trust the teller, trust the tale.' Roth invites us to bypass historical fact and trust his untrustworthy characters – Gabriel Dan and Franz Tunda, the returning Russian prisoners of war, Friedrich Kargan the revolutionary agent provocateur, Eibenschütz the inspector of weights and measures, Kapturak the moneylender and people-trafficker, Fallmerayer the stationmaster and Golubchik the political assassin. They each reinvent themselves in order to take their place in a fluid world. And to do so, they must all cross borders, either through compulsion, choice, profession or passion.

Visiting Western Ukraine in the early twenty-first century one can see how little has changed in Roth's smudged birthplace. Seventy years after his death it is once again the natural habitat of the displaced. Hitler may have removed all of the Jews and Stalin most of the Poles and Romanians but others have taken their place. Since the collapse of the Soviet Union Ukraine has been a soft border for economic migrants and sex-traffickers, just as it was when Jadlowker's tavern was a place of passage on the Tsarist frontier. It is the same covert marketplace for decommissioned weapons as it was when Tunda and Kargan smuggled bombs and small arms past the border guards for their revolutionary colleagues. It is also a huge factory for computer viruses, some of which are designed to destabilise entire economies. If we find some of Roth's plotlines far-fetched, we only have to export them into Moldova or Belorus or any other remnant of the USSR to see the consequences of displacement after an empire dies. When Ukraine turned its back on the Soviet Empire to the east, correspondents observed agents provocateurs pouring into frontier cities. The shouts of freedom in the baroque squares of Lviv echoed northwards into the Baltic states and south into Ossetia and Georgia. But as Joseph Roth revealed eight decades earlier, such newly discovered liberties are often paper-thin. Since the Orange Revolution, Ukraine has drifted backwards and forwards between Russia and the west, compelled by its historic identity as the land 'by the border'.

This constant sense of being stranded between somewhere and nowhere goes some way towards explaining the elusive nature of Roth's fiction. It also explains another paradox which has puzzled me ever since I first finished *The Radetzky March* in the mid-1970s. For thirty years I hunted in vain for an English biography or a decent critical study of Roth. My repeated proposals for a documentary film about him were met with a blank stare. Outside continental Europe he had slipped under the radar. How could an author whose work has been filmed both for cinema and television in Austria, Germany and even Italy, still be so marginalised? How could the best-known journalist writing in German in the 1920s have left no legacy in the Anglophone world? His accounts of political culture in the Weimar Republic and early Soviet Russia are years ahead of their time. Yet he is never mentioned in the two most substantial accounts of Weimar culture, by Peter Gay and John Willett. In his prescient fiction, he warned of the dangers of burgeoning Nazism as early as 1922. So why does hardly anyone read let alone teach *The Spider's Web* or *The Silent Prophet*, which respectively describe the totalitarian threats of fascism and communism?

It was only after the fall of the Berlin Wall that I began to understand the reasons for this neglect. We had simply forgotten the world he evoked. Perhaps, once it emerged from the Soviet ice age which had preserved it for half a century, its most potent chronicler would at last find his proper place. And for a brief moment that seemed possible. The novels and journalism were finally reissued in decent translations. Roth's Galician birthplace even aspired briefly to unity with Western Europe. Then the caravan moved on and its chronicler slipped back into the shadows. But then brevity always was and still remains the fate of Roth's unstable homeland.

Two

– Kakania and the Emperor's Bust –

I n 2008, for the first time in ninety-four years, you could travel the thousand miles from Trieste to Lviv without a visa. During two world wars and the cold one which followed five new European nation states were born, shattered, reborn and destroyed once again. With every death and rebirth, new frontiers were drawn and new customs posts erected; new border guards put on new uniforms and new immigration documents were printed. At the turn of the new millennium these recreated nations were joined in a single political unit. Hungary, Poland and Czechoslovakia were welcomed into the European Union, closely followed by Slovenia and Romania. Croatia and Bosnia hammered impatiently on the door.

Waiting in the anteroom, with the encouragement of the United States and to the annoyance of Russia, was the Ukrainian homeland of Joseph Roth. The Habsburg Crown Lands, which had seemed confined to the dustbin of history after the peace settlements of Versailles and Saint Germain, were once more part of a contiguous Europe. Another treaty now ensured free passage across former frontiers. It was forged not in the aftermath of war but peacefully in a boring little town in neutral Luxembourg called Schengen. To be sure, the journey from the Adriatic to the Carpathians still has its delays and interruptions. If you wish to travel from Franz Joseph's only seaport to the edge of Russia your train must still pass through Poland, Hungary or Romania. You are then brought up short at the Ukrainian border in the middle of the night for three passport checks and a three-hour wait while the carriage wheels are rolled out from under you and replaced by a new set. The former Soviet Union and Europe may have kissed and made up but they have not got round to reconciling their railway gauges. Nevertheless, if you are a European citizen, once your papers are returned by the boot-faced border guards, you are safe to continue to the edge of the Russian Federation without producing any other documents or paying a single penny, euro, zloty or forint.

Crossing this newly loosened Mitteleuropa in the spring of 2010, I was reminded of Count Morstin's impressions of it in Roth's novella. Fifty years of somnolent communism had preserved an imperial landscape which had largely disappeared west of Prague. It was still possible to see the Austro-Hungarian Empire replicated in every corner of every province. Roth's description of it in *The Bust of the Emperor* is composed of tiny banal details and each one is a miniature map of the whole, like a piece of fractal geometry:

As he travelled around the centre of his multitudinous father-land, what he responded to most were certain specific and unmistakeable manifestations that recurred in their unvarying and still colourful fashion, on every railway station, every kiosk, every public building, every school and church in the Crown Lands of the Empire. All over the policemen wore the same feathered hats or ochre helmets with golden pompoms and glittering Habsburg double eagles; all over, the wooden doors of the K and K Trafik stores were painted in black and yellow diagonals . . . All over there were the same coffee houses with vaulted smoky ceilings, with dark alcoves, where chess players sat hunkered like alert fowls, with bars full of multi-coloured bottles and sparkling glasses, presided over by bosomy blonde barmaids . . .

Morstin's image of his lost fatherland as a 'mansion with many doors' is both nostalgic and oddly prophetic. During the Cold War, the idea of a single geo-political umbrella sheltering all the Central European nation states seemed both absurd and vaguely threatening. However, in 1999, when I interviewed Prince Karel Schwarzenberg, the current Czech foreign minister and great-great-great-nephew of Franz Joseph's prime minister, his description of the European Union echoed Morstin's words. Schwarzenberg believed that only through interdependence could the fragmented nations of Mitteleuropa avoid the horrors which followed the dismantling of the Habsburg Empire: 'I fear that if the aspirant nations are not admitted to the EU, the fate that we prepared for them in the twentieth century will be visited on them in the twenty-first.'

There is another echo here – of a warning delivered a hundred and fifty years earlier. It may well have been a conscious echo because its author was another Schwarzenberg – the son and successor of Franz Joseph's prime minister. In the 1880s, he warned the Czech nationalists in the Austrian parliament that Austria's enemies would be only too happy to see the Empire decompose into its constituent parts. The small states which made up Austria-Hungary were symbiotic with Vienna. If they uncoupled, like my railway carriage at the Ukrainian border, they would be cast adrift: 'If you and yours hate this state, what will you do with your country, which is too small to stand alone? Will you give it to Germany or to Russia, for you have no choice if you abandon the Austrian Union.'

The symbiosis between Franz Joseph's scattered 'peoples' and their imperial protector is a recurrent theme in Roth's fiction, particularly in the novels written during his years of exile. For the Trottas and Count Morstin and Captain Taittinger and all the other Austro-Hungarian bit players in his stories, the survival of the Habsburg monarchy through four centuries of European conflict and bloodshed was living proof that it was indeed greater than the sum of its parts. Roth's vision of the Empire is spiritual as well as political. It digs down to the imperial collective memory and unearths its origins in the mission of medieval Austria to be the guardian of Christian Europe. In *The Radetzky March* this idea is a counterweight to his melancholy chronicle of the two final Habsburg decades. His own attitude towards it in the novel remains ambivalent – both affectionate and despairing. He portrays a family of nations defined by the very forces which are pulling it apart. On the one hand the Habsburg Empire's strength is in its diversity. On the other that diversity is destroying it. At the climax of *The Radetzky March* on the eve of the Great War, Roth inserts a meditation on the nature of the Empire. To emphasise the paradox of Austria-Hungary he places his description of this uneasy compromise between nationalism and dynasticism in the mouth not of an Austrian but a Pole – Trotta's friend Count Chojnicki:

As we speak it's falling apart. It's already fallen apart! An old man with not long to go, a head cold could finish him off, he keeps his throne by the simple miracle that he's still able to sit on it. But how much longer, how much longer? The age doesn't want us any more! The age wants us to establish autonomous nation states . . . Our Monarchy is founded on faith and devotion; on the belief that God has chosen the Habsburgs to reign over a certain number of Christian peoples. Our emperor is like a worldly Pope.

There is a huge amount of Habsburg symbolism packed into that short paragraph. Chojnicki links the fragility of the Empire to the physical weakness of its ruler. The only power which can override his frailty is the power of the Christian faith. The Kaiser has been chosen as the custodian of Christendom – as the Count describes him a 'worldly Pope'. This comparison is not accidental. It harks back to the Empire's glory days in the sixteenth and seventeenth centuries. The historian Andrew Wheatcroft, in his study of imperial iconography *The Habsburgs: Embodying Empire*, describes how the dynasty co-opted Christian symbolism to justify its rise from a minor Alpine family into Europe's mightiest power. This was demonstrated in the comic opera of Austria's celebrated triumph over the Turks at the siege of Vienna in 1683. During the conflict the Habsburg Emperor Leopold absented himself from the battlefield and victory was actually secured by Polish troops commanded by King John Sobieski. Nevertheless, Leopold insisted on snatching the credit and commissioned a gold inscription to be placed above the gates of the city bearing the following words:

By the Sanctity and Liberality of Pope Innocent XII, by the Counsel and Industry of the August Emperor Leopold I . . . Happy AUSTRIA, for which God always doth wonders against the Turks and the French, arises from her Ashes and after Devastation TRIUMPHS.

When Roth chooses a Pole to describe the crisis facing the monarchy in 1914 he is both echoing Habsburg iconography and undermining it. Chojnicki invokes Catholic Austria's manifest destiny in front of an officer corps made up of Hungarians and Czechs. This little scene is a travesty by parallel – a farcical way of showing how the multicultural kingdom has been fatally compromised by agreeing to share dominion with the Catholic nations which flank it. As Trotta's multicultural fellow soldiers squabble among themselves, they reveal the Habsburg dream unravelling.

Roth is equally ironic when he describes Count Morstin's affectionate tour of his homeland in *The Bust of the Emperor*. It is another comic riff on Habsburg symbology. The imperial emblem of the double-headed eagle, facing west towards France and east towards Ottoman Turkey, is reduced to the feathered headgear of the local police. The letters KK, which stand for the words *Königlich/Kaiserlich* – Imperial/Royal – are embossed not on palaces or town halls but on cafés and tobacconists. Once again, Roth simultaneously celebrates and undermines the Empire. In fact this heroic cryptogram symbolised Austria's last and most desperate attempt to maintain its hegemony in Central Europe. The two letters were attached to every public building and private business following the historic compromise agreed between Austria and Hungary in 1867. The previous year Austria had been defeated by the Prussians at the battle of Königgrätz and suddenly Franz Joseph and his ministers were confronted with a seemingly insoluble conundrum. Austria had lost the leadership of German-speaking Europe. How was she to avoid being absorbed into a greater German state? Even if she succeeded against the power of Prussia, there was a further threat. How could she escape being eroded and bankrupted by her straggling polyglot Eastern dependencies? The solution was to give partial independence to the Hungarians and their own dependent peoples in Croatia, Slovakia and parts of Transylvania. Following this re-marriage of convenience (in German it is called the *Ausgleich*, or compromise) the Hungarian nobility were allowed to control taxation, domestic law and economic policy, while foreign affairs and the army were directed from Vienna's Hofburg. By merging the Crown Lands of Austria and Hungary they could be reborn as a larger composite state. At one and the same time Austria-Hungary could be both an empire and a kingdom.

Describing this Dual Monarchy is a frustrating exercise. Part of it was made up of family possessions, lands which the Habsburgs had inherited largely through dynastic marriage. The other half was an ancient empire, jealously defended as the successor to Charlemagne's Holy Roman Empire. The Habsburg family gained the imperial crown in the late Middle Ages not through marriage but by the electoral vote of the German-speaking nobility who owned most of Europe east of the Alps. They baptised themselves in grandiose language as the *Heilige Romische Reich, Deutsche Nazion*. According to the old schoolboy joke it was neither holy, Roman nor an empire. By the time of the *Ausgleich* it was not even a German nation. More than half of its subjects were Magyars and Slavs. As a result Austria-Hungary ended up with one foot in the sixteenth century and the Catholic West and the other in the nineteenth century and the Orthodox East. The identity of the Kaiser was equally schizophrenic. When he was in Vienna, he was Franz Joseph the Habsburg Emperor. When he was crowned in the ancient Magyar capital of Pozony – today's Bratislava – he was called Ferenc Joszef, King of Hungary. The Kaiser's multiple personality disorder was diagnosed by Roth's fellow novelist Robert Musil. While Roth saw the Empire as a melancholy farce, Musil presented it as theatre of the absurd. At the beginning of his huge unfinished novel *The Man Without Qualities* – a blend of philosophy, satire and speculation – he improvised on the German pronunciation of the letters KK and re-christened the Empire *Kakania*. 'Kaka' is also the nursery word for excrement, and Musil's Austria-Hungary was the kingdom of crap.

It is interesting to compare how Musil and Roth characterise the bi-polar monarchy. The two novelists were almost exact contemporaries, although

Musil was born fourteen years earlier and survived Roth by a decade. They each chose to write about the Empire several years after it came to an end, but although they were both preoccupied with the reasons for its collapse they approach it from opposite directions. Musil's vision is centripetal; he examines the culture of Kakania through a microscope. Roth is centrifugal; he watches the Empire fall apart from its distant margins. Musil was an engineer by training and his language is quasi-scientific. Every word is weighed and every phenomenon tested to destruction. Roth began as a popular journalist with a sideline in atmospheric travel writing and he is anything but analytical. His style is sometimes poetic and dreamlike, often dark and threatening. When Musil anatomises the Habsburg zeitgeist, he offers us a medical report:

There is just something missing in everything; though you can't put your finger on it, as if there had been a change in the blood or in the air; a mysterious disease has eaten away the previous period's seeds of genius, but everything sparkles with novelty and finally one has no way of knowing whether the world has really grown worse or oneself merely older.

When Roth observes the same phenomena his words are almost Gothic. He could be describing the paintings of those earlier Habsburg artists Bosch and Breughel which paper the walls of Vienna's *Kunsthistorisches Museum*:

. . . none of the officers of his Apostolic Majesty knew that over the glass bumpers from which they drank death had already crossed his bony invisible hands.

Musil diagnoses a disease of the blood; Roth already feels the chill of the bone.

The contrast between centripetal Musil and centrifugal Roth is evident on every page. Musil has little interest in Austria-Hungary's remote provinces. In the first two thirds of *The Man Without Qualities* scarcely a paragraph ventures outside Vienna. Even in the final unfinished chapters, which open with the provincial funeral of the hero Ulrich's father, only a handful of sentences tell us that we have left Vienna and are now in a region where both German and Slav languages are spoken. For the rest of its 1,800 pages, Kakania is presented not as a grand cosmopolis, let alone a mighty kingdom but as a laboratory. On the single occasion when one of Musil's characters reflects on the nature of the Dual Monarchy, it is like reading a mathematical treatise:

The Austrian existed only in Hungary and there as an object of dislike; at home he called himself a national of the kingdoms and lands of the Austro-Hungarian Monarchy as represented in the Imperial Council, meaning that he was an Austrian plus a Hungarian minus that Hungarian . . .

The crisis of nationality which finally destroyed the Dual Monarchy is rarely mentioned. In Kakania,

Hungarians, Poles, Czechs, Romanians, Ruthenians and South Slavs are all but invisible. Austrian Jews are even more marginalised. There is only one Jewish character in the entire book – a Galician lady's maid called Rachel who, after the birth of her illegitimate child, is charitably taken into domestic service by a society hostess. Following her first appearance, Rachel vanishes for 300 pages and returns briefly only to spy on her employers and to be almost impregnated a second time. Jews as an ethnic group are awarded one brief and perplexing mention in the book's unfinished second part, where Musil stages a debate about whether they should embrace their alien status or quietly assimilate. Like every other political discussion in the novel, it strolls around for a few pages and then runs into the sand. The kingdom of Kakania itself is an intellectual construct rather than a physical space. It is a metropolitan debating chamber peopled by prosperous sophisticates.

Nothing could be further from Roth's fractured kingdom of the displaced. Few of his principal characters are native Germans. They have surnames like Pum and Dan and Pansin and Tunda. They live in Schmerinka, Zuchnow, Koropta and Zlotogrod. Vienna is a refuge or a place of passage, rarely a home. With the exception of his late novel *The Tale of the 1002nd Night* (published in the UK under the title *The String of Pearls*), the only time we witness imperial grandeur is in the short chapter in *The Radetzky March* where Trotta and his mistress visit the capital city during the Corpus Christi celebrations. Here the grandson of the hero of Solferino watches the annual procession with the eyes of provincial tourist and Roth suddenly reverts to the style of his own travel journalism and *Feuilletons*. He paints a magical urban landscape in order to contrast it with the muddy reality of the distant provinces:

The inhabitants of this city, cheerful subjects of His Apostolic Majesty, members virtually of his household, thronged the entire Ringstrasse. The whole city was like an extended court. In the arcades of the ancient palaces stood the liveried porters with their staffs of office, mighty gods among the lackeys.

The two novelists could be describing completely different empires a thousand miles apart. They each observe a world which has expended its moral capital but they come to opposite conclusions. Musil's hollowed-out society is composed of pointless committee meetings, feverish theorising and confused political rhetoric. His characters are on a frustrated quest for something to transcend their daily lives. He is far more concerned with their inner landscape than with the real world outside the windows of their comfortable homes in Vienna's First District or the Höhe Warte. His neurasthenic socialites have run out of spiritual steam. Their dialogue may be informed by the ideas which were being born in Vienna at the turn of the twentieth century – the polemics of Karl Kraus, the psychology of Sigmund Freud and the philosophy of Ludwig Wittgenstein. However, Musil's narrative floats above the everyday reality of a city which was experiencing poverty and prostitution on an industrial scale. In contrast, Roth's characters live in a world of soup kitchens and strikes, revolutionary cadres and political prisons. Where Musil is detached, Roth is always engaged. While Musil observes Austria's identity crisis only in passing, Roth picks at it like a scab. Time and again he traces it to the contradictions which lie beneath the ethnic equilibrium which Franz Joseph and his ministers struggled so hard to maintain in the decades after the *Ausgleich*.

This is nowhere more evident than in the tragicomic climax of *The Radetzky March*. As we observed earlier, it is set during the summer of 1914 at the party organised in his castle by Count Chojnicki to conclude manoeuvres in the Galician garrison where Carl Joseph Trotta has chosen to serve. The action is fuelled, as so often in Roth, by insecurity and alcohol. While the Slavs and Czechs and Hungarians bicker among themselves, an ensign arrives to announce the assassination in Sarajevo of the heir to throne. As the news penetrates their clouded brains, the party disintegrates into a screaming match:

Then Herr von Babenhausen, Master of the Horse with the Reserve, got involved . . .

'Bosnia's a long way from here. We don't care about any rumours. I shit on rumours! We'll learn soon enough anyway.'

'Bravo!' called out Baron Nagy Jenö, one of the Hussars. Even though he was indisputably descended from a Jewish grandfather in Ödenberg, and the barony had only been purchased in his father's time, he was convinced that the Magyars were one of the most aristocratic races in the Monarchy . . .

First Lieutenant Kinsky, born and bred on the Moldau, claimed that the heir to the succession represented only a rather slim chance for the Monarchy . . .

In this scene, Roth exposes the contradictions within Franz Joseph's multicultural experiment not by debating them but by turning them into farce. The 'historic compromise' which united twelve disparate ethnic groups is not a force for stability; it is a source of paralysis. The constituent parts of the Empire now cancel each other out. In a Polish castle, peopled by Germans, Czechs, Slovenes and Hungarians, Roth satirises the confusion of politicians and generals on all sides on the eve of the Great War. There is a similar passage in A. J. P. Taylor's celebrated monograph on the origins of the conflict, *War by Timetable*:

In this way, almost a month passed. The Archduke had been assassinated. Austria-Hungary took no action, even diplomatic. The question was not quite forgotten in the other European capitals but it lost any sense of urgency. Most people assumed that the Austrians would do nothing serious in their usual way.

Taylor's description of Europe's leaders stumbling myopically into battle could have been inserted into the pages of *The Radetzky March*. Those who dismiss Roth's vision of the end of the Empire as a blend of sentiment and cynicism, a kind of Mahler symphony in prose, forget that the novel was written shortly after he had published some of the most trenchant political essays of the 1920s. When dealing with recent history Roth the journalist and Roth the novelist sing from the same score.

There is one further element which sets Roth apart from most of his literary contemporaries. Because he observes the Empire from its eastern edge, the Slavs and Magyars and Germans who take centre stage are joined by a supporting cast of rural Jews. If you enter Roth's world through the gateway of *The Radetzky March* it is easy to overlook them. Although more than a third of the novel is set in the Empire's most Jewish province, Galician Jews, who made up more than 30 per cent of the region's population in 1914, are largely absent. There is one important exception. When Franz Joseph visits his frontier provinces he has a private conversation with a rabbi who prophesies that he will not live 'to see the end of the world'. It is a touching and memorable moment but it is about the Emperor, not his interlocutor. Otherwise the only Jew featured in the novel is the trafficker and moneylender Kapturak, who is the sinister catalyst for Trotta's drunken decline into debt and his role is functional rather than thematic. However, Jews play a much more significant role in the later works, particularly those written during his Parisian exile. Here they are largely presented retrospectively, their life and culture preserved in the aspic of Roth's Brody childhood in the 1890s. *Job* and *Leviathan* are both set in Galician *stetls* at the end of the nineteenth century. They are sometimes written off as yet more sentimental fables but their surface texture is misleading. In their different way they share a great deal with the more visceral political fiction of the 1920s. Like the returning soldiers, vagabonds and political adventurers in his earlier stories, Roth's Jews play a social as well as a narrative role. They are extra-territorial and supranational. They are as much the product of the Empire as the Hungarians, Czechs and Slovenes in *The Radetzky March*. They define Habsburg society by being both outside and inside it.

Their ambivalent status was another consequence of the political upheavals of 1867. When the Dual Monarchy was established, the Hofburg introduced a more liberal constitution. This was initially to satisfy the demands of the Czechs and South Slavs who mistrusted the newly empowered Hungarian nobility. A by-product of this settlement was that

Habsburg Jews were no longer confined by law to the borderland *stetls*. They could now live and work in Vienna and Prague and Budapest and for the first time they could contribute to Austrian political life. However, unlike the Moravians or Croats or Transylvanians, they lacked a homeland, even a potential one. They were only protected by being citizens of the composite monarchy. When that collapsed, they were cut adrift. Roth describes this in his collection of essays *The Wandering Jews*, published three years before *The Radetzky March*:

Every nationality within Austria-Hungary pressed its claim on the basis of its 'territory'. Only the Jews . . . had no territory of their own. In Galicia the majority of them were neither Poles nor Ruthenians. However, anti-Semitism was to be found equally among Germans and Czechs, Poles and Ruthenians, Magyars and Romanians in Transylvania. They managed to refute the proverb that says that when two quarrel, the third is always the winner. The Jews were always the third party and they always lost.

This is another prophecy and not just because it pre-echoes the fate of Austrian Jewry after the *Anschluss*. Jews were not alone in their post-war homelessness. All the Central European nation states created in 1918 contained linguistic and ethnic minorities squeezed uncomfortably behind new borders. Hungarian-speakers in Romania, Sudeten Germans, Slovaks and Romanians in Western

Ukraine and Slovenes in Austrian Carinthia remained extra-territorial up to, during and after the Second World War. They were also 'third parties' and they too 'always lost'. Jews were simply the most visible example of the newly stateless of Mitteleuropa.

Their displacement was not confined to the 1920s. It was extended and intensified in 1945 when the Russians 'liberated' Southern Poland, Hungary, Czechoslovakia, Romania, Yugoslavia and Western Ukraine. Its consequences are still with us today. In redrawing the map of Europe the Soviets cared little for people's ethnic origins. Whole national communities were transplanted as far as Siberia and the Caucasus. In the USSR, political loyalty replaced national identity. This was equally true in those communities who remained in their homelands. The various puppet regimes installed by Stalin in Central and South-East Europe swept their national minorities under the carpet.

I witnessed this at first hand during my earlier travels through Franz Joseph's former Crown Lands. I met Hungarian-speakers in Cluj who considered themselves marginalised by the Romanian state when it was enlarged to include Transylvania. In Bukovina I was introduced to Romanian speakers who faced discrimination when it was incorporated into Western Ukraine. The same was true of Ruthenes in Slovakia, Slovaks in the Czech lands and Roma gypsies everywhere. Most of all it festered in the composite state of former Yugoslavia, which was as much a construct under Marshal Tito in the 1950s as it had been when it was invented by Woodrow Wilson in 1918. In the South Slav lands national rivalries were put into the deep freeze for thirty-five years under communism, but when Tito died some very nasty nationalist organisms crawled out of the icebox. The principal victims were the Bosnian Moslems who, like Roth's wandering Jews, were 'lost third parties' and were squeezed between Catholic Croats to the west and Orthodox Serbs to the east.

The fate of the Bosniaks closely mirrors that of the Empire's eastern Jews. They were originally Ottoman subjects who became Habsburg citizens when Bosnia was annexed by Austria in 1908. For the next eighty years, they were passed from hand to hand as Bosnia was successively incorporated into the Kingdom of Serbs, Croats and Slovenes after the Treaty of Trianon and then into Tito's Yugoslavia after the Second World War. When that nation also fell apart in 1992 they were attacked by militant nationalists on every side. When I visited Bosnia after the Dayton 'peace settlement' of 1995, the late Marion Wenzel, director of Bosnia-Herzegovina Heritage Rescue, unconsciously echoed Roth's thoughts in *The Wandering Jews* seventy years earlier:

When I came to Bosnia at the beginning of the war in 1993, I was told: 'We Moslems don't have a country to look to as our "friendly outside land." The Serbs have Serbia and the Croatians have Croatia. But we really look to the Habsburg Empire.' I thought: 'This is pretty queer.'

Queer indeed to describe the wars in former Yugoslavia as a consequence of the collapse of Austria-Hungary. However, it confirms that Roth's centrifugal vision of the Habsburg Empire as a 'mansion with many doors' was still valid almost a century later. Roth believed passionately that the future of Mitteleuropa was multicultural. His comfortable melting pot is in huge contrast to the centripetal Kakania which Musil evoked in the years immediately after the Treaty of Versailles. Musil could only imagine the afterlife of the Crown Lands in ethnic German terms. In his eyes, the heterogeneous Habsburg Crown Lands could never provide a model for European integration. In 1919, in an essay written well before the Kakania chapter of *The Man Without Qualities*, he even proposed a linguistic and cultural *Anschluss* between rump Austria and the now reduced Germany. He described Austria as a 'petrified illusion'. He dismissed the concept of Austro-Hungarian culture as a myth and blamed Austria's collapse on the failure of Habsburg multiculturalism. Only through the German language could Austria regain its cultural confidence. In the 1920s, when Austria and Germany were both briefly social democracies, there might have been some weight to his argument. After the conflagration of the Second World War it is Roth's spacious mansion which seems prophetic and Musil's German-speaking confederation which now looks dangerously sentimental.

When he wrote *The Bust of the Emperor* in the mid-1930s, Roth was flirting with the Catholic monarchism of his fellow Austrian exiles. Count Morstin's panegyric for the old Empire, like Chojnicki's, takes refuge in Habsburg religious iconography:

No human virtue can endure in this world, save only one; true piety. Belief can cause us no disappointment since it promises us nothing in this world. The true believer does not fail us, for he seeks no recompense on earth. If one uses the same yardstick for peoples, it implies that they seek in vain for national virtues, so called, and that these are even more questionable than human virtues. For this reason, I hate nationalism and nation states.

Roth published his novella in 1935, when the consequences of nationalism were already there for anyone with eyes to see. However, Hitler's Reich and Stalin's Soviet Union combined to anaesthetise cultural identity for a further half century. Roth's multicultural model had to wait another sixty years before it could be built over the ruins of the Berlin Wall and in the ashes of the Warsaw Pact. Even then in today's Galicia, Bukovina and Moldova the questions he asked seventy-five years ago still remain unanswered and their citizens are once more on the move. If they are lucky, they are migrant workers in the factories of Frankfurt or the cafés of Manchester or the hotels of Brussels. Roth would have recognised them as he scribbled at his *stammtisch* in his favourite Berlin *kneipe* or at the corner table at the Café Tournon. He might also have noticed the frightened scrawny girls from Moldova and Montenegro trafficked across the Schengen borders by latter-day Kapturaks with their stolen passports secreted in their attaché cases. Roth's extra-territorials and their exploiters who made their first appearance on the top floors of Hotel Savoy in 1923 were still sitting at the bar nearly twenty years later in *The Capuchin Crypt*. When I checked into the Hotel Zhorzh in Lviv in 2001, the pink stucco was cracked and the silent lifts had broken down but the currency dealers were still whispering by the reception desk and stateless teenage girls with ancient eyes were still turning tricks over warm Russian champagne.

Extra-territoriality is a constant in Roth's fiction. It is the mirror he holds up to his times and the glass in which he inspects himself. The 'silent prophet' Kargan, the accidental assassin Golubchik and the perpetual refugee Franz Tunda may fetch up in almost every European capital city, but each of these wanderers is rooted in the Ukrainian borderlands. They are all displaced people, alter egos of their creator, Moses Joseph Roth, the greatest shape-changer of them all.

Three

– Extra-territorial –

N
o one knows for certain how many refugees there were in Europe and Russia at the time of the armistice in 1918. Every historian and social scientist seems to use a different yardstick. In his magisterial survey *The Short Twentieth Century* E. J. Hobsbawm suggests that at the end of the Great War there were between four and five million displaced persons in continental Europe alone. Peter Gatrell in *A Whole Empire Walking* records a further 3.3 million refugees in Russia in the year 1915, rising to more than six million by 1917. This would mean that on the eve of the Revolution refugees not only made up at least 5 per cent of the total Russian population but actually outnumbered her industrial proletariat.

These numbers may seem unremarkable when compared with those rendered homeless during the Shoah, in the Gulags and after the Soviet conquest of Eastern Europe. Yet for Joseph Roth and his contemporaries the displacement of millions across the frontiers of Russia, Poland and Austria-Hungary between 1918 and 1920 was shocking and totally unprecedented. Nothing like it had been seen for centuries. Even the Crimean and Franco-Prussian Wars left the populations of Central Europe largely undisturbed. One has to go back to the religious wars of the mid-1600s to witness dislocation on an equivalent scale. As a result, most of the politicians, philosophers and creative artists of the 1920s lacked the intellectual equipment to comprehend the flood of stateless humanity which swept across Eastern Europe after the surrender of the Central Powers.

It is hardly surprising that homelessness is central to Roth's imaginative world. There is scarcely a single work written during the 1920s without a refugee or stateless wanderer somewhere in the dramatis personae. From the moment he settled in Vienna, throughout his travels in Germany and Russia and right up to his final exile in Paris, he was surrounded by extra-territorials. His early political fiction is packed with border-crossing transients; returning prisoners of war like Gabriel Dan and Franz Tunda, or spies, mercenaries and criminals like Joseph Kargan, Tarabas and Kapturak. The fables written in France in the 1930s treat the subject more gently but they also frequently revolve around characters' impulsive decisions to leave familiar homelands. Stationmaster Fallmerayer follows his enigmatic Russian countess from Ruthenia in the First World War to the south of France. Eibenschütz, the exemplary inspector of weights and measures, leaves his dull and comfortable home to live among the itinerant gypsies, Jews, coachmen and smugglers of the frontier taverns. In these stories transience is hard-wired into the human condition. Even when their displacement is the result of accident, it still frames every event in their lives. When Carl Joseph von Trotta in *The Radetzky March* is compelled to abandon his Moravian regiment he chooses a god-forsaken garrison in Galicia. Superficially the fact that he places himself on the fault line between the German and Slavic worlds seems strangely arbitrary. Yet it allows him to observe momentous events through Roth's characteristic inverted spyglass. At the end of the novel Roth finally describes the crisis in Sarajevo in August 1914 but only from a distance of a thousand kilometres and after a hundred pages in which nothing significant happens. At Chojnicki's party, the assassination of Franz Ferdinand is announced almost as an afterthought. Like most of Roth's mature fiction, it mixes the accidental and the momentous with apparent disregard.

This is another product of Roth's centrifugal temperament. He observes great events from the edge of the world and reflects them in the arbitrary fate of insignificant nations and individuals. It is difficult to believe that a writer like Musil or Schnitzler, brought up in urbane imperial Vienna, would assemble such an undistinguished cast of characters as the drifters who people *The Radetzky March* or *The Capuchin Crypt*. Throughout his creative life

Roth's fiction is dominated by society's waifs and strays. Even when he passed through the capital city after the Great War and adopted the dress and manners of a metropolitan dandy, he still chose to write about the turning points of modern Europe from the perspective of the dispossessed. The seventh storey of the strange labyrinthine Hotel Savoy houses all the refuse of post-imperial Mitteleuropa at the turn of the 1920s. His cast is composed of third-rate vaudeville artistes, petty traders, low-grade lottery speculators, stateless returning soldiers and former prisoners of war. Like those other Habsburg provincials Kafka and Capek, he invents a world controlled by distant and anonymous forces. In *Hotel Savoy* the powers that be are literally invisible. The hotel manager Kalegouropoulos is always on the point of appearing but like Beckett's Godot he never arrives. We never know the real reason for the industrial strife or the larger social consequences of the recent war. Like Joseph K or Rusum's robots, his characters are the blind puppets of careless fortune.

What really concerns Roth are not the great political movements of post-war Eastern Europe but the desperate and often feeble strategies his characters employ to circumvent them. His protagonists are the casualties of a war which seems to persist long after the ink on the peace treaties has dried. They have fetched up in the Hotel Savoy because no one and nowhere else will shelter them. The tone is set in Gabriel Dan's declaration in its opening page:

'I am thankful once again to strip off an old life, as I so often have during these years. I look back upon a soldier, a murderer, a man almost murdered, a man resurrected, a prisoner, a wanderer.'

When he hooks up with a former comrade, the would-be revolutionary Zwonimir Pansin, the two of them conclude that the war will never end. When they do find a temporary refuge they are still victims of chance. Their fellow guests on the upper floors of the hotel usually arrive destitute. From time to time some of them experience unearned good fortune, but it is almost always short-lived. Like the disgraced clerk Isidor Schabel, most of them are trapped in a downward spiral:

He had once been a notary in Romania but because of embezzlement has ceased to be a notary. This is already his sixth year of living in the Hotel Savoy . . . He eked out a living by doing hole-and-corner scribe's work . . .

The identity of the city where *Hotel Savoy* is set is deliberately concealed. It is clearly in Eastern Europe but its social fabric has more in common with the feverish atmosphere of the Weimar Republic. The novella inhabits a strange composite of Lwow and Lodz after the end of the war and Berlin in the early

1920s. The dancers and war cripples who crowd its pages are the prose equivalents of the figures in *Cirkus* and *Der Krieg,* the lithographs produced by Otto Dix in Berlin three years earlier. They could also be minor characters in the films which Murnau and Pabst were directing in the UFA studios a few kilometres away in Babelsberg. In an essay on film in the *Frankfurter Zeitung*, published in 1925, Roth praises the UFA aesthetic of 'romantic irony' – a description which might equally be applied to his own work. The fantasists and speculators who inhabit the Hotel Savoy could have walked straight out of Murnau's sad satire *Der Letzte Mann*, which depicts the decline and fall of a hotel doorman.

Yet there is something which sets Roth's characters apart – their hypnotised fatalism. The Great War has paralysed their will. Far from being a turning point in the history of Eastern Europe, it is a kind of spiritual Groundhog Day. Are we in 1924 during the economic collapse or are we trapped on the Russian frontier in a never-ending repetition of 1916? There are strikes and grotesque levels of inflation but on the edge of frame there are also perpetual waves of returning soldiery and refugees:

They come in groups, many at a time. They come in shoals, like certain fish at certain times of the year. They flow westwards, these returning soldiers. For two months there were none to be seen. Then week after week they flow past out of Russia and Siberia and the border countries.

Eastern Europe is perpetually swamped by the stateless:

This bewildered, irritated, exhausted crowd spreads like a continuous flood along the roads, obstructing military transport and bringing complete chaos . . . This human mass is pouring across Russia in a broad wave.

This passage is not from *Hotel Savoy* or anything else by Roth. It is a direct quotation from a report by the Tsar's Deputy Chief of Chancery A. N. Iachontov in 1915, when the refugee crisis was paralysing all the nations bordering Russia, including the eastern edges of Austria-Hungary. In 1916 more than 400,000 Galician refugees poured into Volhynia, and the waves of the displaced did not end with Russia's exit from the Great War.

The title of Roth's next novel, *Flight Without End*, might stand for much of Eastern Europe in 1919. Its suspension of time and its blurred montage of fact and invention suggest the aesthetic of Germany's New Objectivity, but like Weimar cinema and graphics its prose is neither documentary nor coldly objective. It floats above history, describing the effects of post-war displacement from the inside outwards. Nor is the narrative confined to the years of conflict; it bleeds into the ensuing decade. Like Georg Grosz's disturbing sketches of Berlin street life in the early 1920s, Roth is preoccupied with effects rather than causes. He observes how the war has bred mutations in the European psyche and how homelessness has now become almost a way of life. He describes the returning soldiers as 'tramps, who have brushed against many lives' and wonders whether 'they would not have been happier staying on in the big world rather than returning to the small home of wife, child and fireside'. Here he differs from his German contemporaries. His characters have gone beyond history; they have embraced their fate. Like his later creations Fallmerayer and Eibenschütz (or like Roth himself), they have become wanderers by choice.

In *Hotel Savoy* Gabriel Dan compares his own voluntary displacement to the desultory ambience of a railway station where he is a perpetual passenger. Apart from his compulsion to move on, Dan also exhibits a fractured sense of personal identity – another recurrent feature in Roth's work. When the nervous young dancer Stasia, first heard pacing the room above his own, asks Gabriel whether he is a fellow 'artiste', his reply could be the motto of a whole generation:

'No. I don't know what I am. Earlier on I wanted to be a writer, but I went to the war and now I feel there is no point in writing. I am a solitary person and cannot write for the public.'

Dan's spiritual vacuum is mirrored in the lost identity of the borderlands themselves. The nameless city in which *Hotel Savoy* takes place could be Lviv or Tarnopol or Czernowitz or any former eastern frontier city cut off from its now defunct imperial hinterland. When Roth returned to Galicia after the war, not only had his own capital city Austrian Lemberg been transformed into Polish Lwow; this regional capital of a newly created nation state was now exercising its political muscle by marginalising large segments of its own population. Ruthenes and Jews (and Roth was both) had to choose new identities. This is another reason why, when he was re-designated a Polish citizen in 1919, Roth's prompt reaction was to apply for Austrian citizenship. It was an act of protest against the forcible re-shaping of his world.

He was one of the lucky few who had the freedom to choose an identity and a homeland. In 1918, many former Habsburg subjects found themselves both homeless and stateless. Hungarians in post-war Romania or Germans in the new Czechoslovakia or Ukrainians in what eventually became the Soviet Union were defined by who they were not rather than by who they were. The manufacture of five new post-war nations had an even more significant by-product. In debatable lands like Galicia and Bukovina citizens who wanted a legal identity required a legitimate set of papers. The presence or absence of papers is a leitmotif throughout Roth's work. At the end of Gabriel Dan's westward return from his Siberian imprisonment, he encounters a hostile local police force and reaches unconsciously for his passport. He asks the constant question for all Central Europeans: 'Do I have my passport? Do I exist without it?' The same is true of Joseph Kargan and Andreas Pum and even the pious Hebrew teacher Mendel Singer in *Job*. They cannot move without the appropriate documents. If legitimate papers are not immediately available, then someone must counterfeit them. The means to produce passports confers almost magical powers on those who manufacture them. The smuggler Kapturak appears in five of Roth's novels, sometimes lending money or arranging cross-border transport but always fabricating official papers. He provides the wherewithal for Mendel Singer to reach his family in America, he presides over Joseph Kargan's numerous changes of name and nationality in *The Silent Prophet* and he spirits people across frontiers in both *Weights and Measures* and *The Capuchin Crypt*. He is the high priest of false identity.

The very idea of a passport is a surprisingly recent invention. Like the word 'refugee', the small cardboard-covered identity document was a by-product of the Great War itself. Until the 1850s, on the few occasions when individuals needed to cross imperial frontiers the authorities provided them with temporary letters of transit. With the arrival of rail travel the whole system broke down and most

European countries abandoned passports altogether. It was only when the old empires collapsed that porous borders and the threat of espionage and terrorism changed the very nature of travel. Ordinary citizens were now required to possess permanent proof that they were who they claimed to be.

This is reflected throughout Roth's fiction. His Galicians, Ruthenians, Ukrainians and Bukovinans are constantly seeking new identities to support new lives in new nations. One further factor adds to their problems: many of them are Jewish. This makes them doubly dependent on their papers. In post-war Poland or Russia or Romania Jews were not automatically guaranteed nationality merely because they once lived there on a temporary basis. In the nineteenth century, the majority of Russian and Polish Jews were settled in the narrow strip of land between the two nations known as the Jewish Pale of Settlement. This was abolished by the reforming government of Tsar Alexander II but even this was a mixed blessing. After the Great War, Jews who ended up on the Russian side of the border might find a refuge in Moscow or St Petersburg or Kiev. However, if they were stranded in Poland or Romania or particularly in Ukraine, which during the civil wars in Russia, Galicia and Bukovina in 1918 and 1919 changed hands four times, they had nowhere which they could comfortably call a homeland. As Galicians, they were neither Poles nor Austrians. If they were from Bukovina they belonged neither to Romania nor to emerging Bolshevik Russia. Paradoxically, it was only in the final decades of the former Habsburg Empire as Austrian subjects that they had ever been able to claim Jewish nationality.

This calls to mind Roth's sly comments on Jewish identity in *The Wandering Jews*. Because they were the only nation in the old empire without a geographical homeland, they suffered double discrimination. In his fiction he turns this paradox on its head. Jews are not an exception but an acute case of the general disease of Mitteleuropa. This sickness became critical when Franz Joseph's family of 'peoples' exchanged their subject status for nation states of their own. Those who did not fit in became extra-territorials. All of Roth's displaced characters, haggling and conniving for new identities in the frontier taverns of Galicia and Volhynia, are metaphorical Jews. If this sounds fanciful, an article published in the Russian journal *Itogi Goda* at the end of the Great War draws a similar parallel:

We have created something akin to a new Pale of Settlement, jealously guarded by the relevant authorities. Society has renounced the refugees, as if they were a vile disease that can only be mentioned in private and in hushed tones.

Roth's Jewish borderlanders are not simply local colour, residual memories from his early years in Brody. Kapturak the smuggler and Jadlowker the

innkeeper and Komrower the revolutionary Talmudist all have a precise social function, particularly in a
new and shifting political landscape. His *Ostjuden*,
whether they are traders or pedlars or chestnut-
roasters or coachmen, are expert at slipping across
borders and skilled at hiding suspects and undes-
irables. Most of all they are past masters at conceal-
ing former identities and forging new ones.

In Roth's fiction the personal and the political
meet and identity itself becomes fluid. Sometimes
his characters are robbed or cheated of their official
documents. Occasionally they choose to adopt different personae to protect themselves against real or
imagined enemies. As radicals or spies they falsify
their entire life histories. The one constant in their
lives is the need for a reliable set of papers. They can
survive wars and revolutions but heaven help them
if they mislay their passports or their permits. In
Roth's third novel, *Rebellion*, completed only a few
months after *Hotel Savoy*, the whole narrative re-
volves around the central character's loss of a work
permit. Andreas Pum is a typical anti-hero of the
New Objectivity. He could have walked straight out
of the Berlin Dada exhibition of 1921. He lives in a
capital city which is a conflation of Vienna and Berlin, with a Pestalozzistrasse and a Café Halili. He has
lost a leg in the war and supports himself by playing sentimental tunes on a hurdy-gurdy. His work
permit is his sheet anchor – with it 'a man may walk

serenely through the streets of the world, though they be swarming with policemen.' At the beginning of the novel he has the good fortune to be sheltered by a plump and kindly widow whom he subsequently marries. However, he becomes involved in an argument on a tram with a bad-tempered businessman, the police intervene and he is accused of being a Bolshevik. He raises his crutch and strikes the officer, who then pockets his work permit. From this moment, both his inner and outer identity begin to dissolve. His permit is cancelled; he loses his status as a war veteran and consequently his employment and his home. His wife abandons him and he is incarcerated in a Berlin jail. He swiftly disintegrates physically and mentally.

In many respects *Rebellion* is a characteristic political fable of the period. Pum is second cousin to the pathetic hotel doorman played by Emil Jannings in Murnau's film. His story anticipates the later fiction of Tucholsky and Kästner. Yet although the style and setting breathe 1920s Berlin, there are constant touches which hint that this is the creation of an Austrian Jew from the east. The sentences are terse and vernacular. The chapters are short and the narrative keeps switching from sudden reversals of fortune to stretches of hallucinatory stasis. In this respect *Rebellion* is more like a parable than a conventional novel. The dreamlike debate in a heavenly court which ends the tale is closer in style to the short stories of Sholem Aleichem than it is to any of Roth's Berlin contemporaries. When Pum challenges the justice of his fate, he directly echoes the book of Job:

'Did God live beyond the stars? Could he bear to watch a man's misery and not intervene? What went on behind that icy blue? Was the world ruled by a tyrant whose injustice was as boundless as the heavens themselves?'

When we read his quasi-Hasidic debates with God, *Rebellion* seems at times like an early draft for *Job*, Roth's first great popular success. Although he never suggests that Pum is Jewish, his speech is peppered with Talmudic language. Like his Old Testament model, he is the personification of stoical, uncomprehending endurance. When he realises that by losing his permit he has forfeited not merely his social status but his very existence, he has a vision of descending into penury and madness. Without his permit he feels as if he is adrift on a hostile sea. Job has now become Jonah.

Rebellion is only superficially a product of the New Objectivity. It certainly employs journalistic narrative gestures and sharply observed social detail. Yet like the cinema and visual art of Weimar Berlin, the documentary surface conceals an expressionist core. Roth employs this stylistic trick throughout his next substantial work, *Flight Without End*, where he goes to great lengths to seduce us into believing that we are witnessing unmediated documentary truth. In the Preface, he constructs a mini-manifesto of the *Neue Sachlichkeit*:

I have invented nothing, made up nothing. The question of 'poetic invention' is no longer relevant. Observed fact is all that counts.

These words are a transparent deception. They are the work of '*Muniu faktisch*' – Roth the congenital faker. The novel claims to document the life of a typical extra-territorial in post-war Europe and it draws on Roth's own journalistic experiences of Germany and Russia in the early 1920s. However, the mock-documentary style is dust thrown in the reader's eyes. His real purpose is the exploration of human identity in a mutating world. Tunda is transient by chance and his story is an existential journey from displacement through engagement to disillusionment and loss. Roth even bulks it out with tantalising fragments of his own autobiography. Tunda is described as a 'first lieutenant in the Austrian army', just as Roth himself often claimed to be a Habsburg officer. He introduces himself as the son of an Austrian major and a Polish Jewess (one of Roth's own manufactured identities). He has 'false papers . . . in the name of Baranowicz', was 'born in Lodz and had been invalided out of the Russian army in 1917'. Like Gabriel Dan his goal is to reach a frontier town across the Galician border – this time Shmerinka, another regular location in Roth's fiction – but otherwise 'he had no particular plan'. He is determined to avoid the Revolution, 'and no longer had a home'. In every respect he is a typical survivor of the calamity of 1918, 'without a name, without importance, without rank, without title, without money and without occupation – homeless and stateless'.

He is one of many alter egos constructed by Roth in his early fiction. He is a shape-changer and the product of historical accident just like his creator. He refers repeatedly to the dissolution of his past history and his personal identity. Needless to say, Tunda's multiple personalities and his unreliable personal narrative are reflected in his false documents. During his early months as a tyro revolutionary, he keeps his original passport concealed in his clothes. At an appropriate moment, he slips off the skin of Baranowicz the Pole and replaces it with his former identity as an Austrian officer and Siberian prisoner of war. Arriving at the Austrian consulate in Moscow, he presents a new face, a new voice and a set of papers to match the set of tasks he has been given by the revolutionary cadres. There is something surreal about the way these external signifiers transform his inner self. His name takes on a life of its own and Tunda, 'who had been Baranowicz for several years', sees 'the real Tunda emerge from the document'. As the novel progresses, his personality softens at the edges. He becomes the composite of all his fabrications. He contrasts the apparent solidity of the world he inhabits as a spy and agent provocateur with his own lack of inner substance. He is no longer able to distinguish between the real and the invented – between his own life and the stolen fragments of other people's.

In some respects *Flight Without End* is an imperfect work. Two thirds of the way through it seems to lose its way. As Tunda's personality fragments the narrative breaks up into a string of documentary cameos. Roth himself emerges from behind the scenery and tries to direct the action. He introduces his protagonist to new characters from the artistic salons of Germany and France who might have stepped out of Roth's own *feuilletons*. Over the final thirty pages, both the story and its central character slowly decompose. The novel's own style now reflects the world it inhabits. It is as if the collapse of social and political stability in Europe has undermined the very act of writing.

By the end of the book, when Tunda is left with no visible means of support and no purpose in life, he has become the personification of a lost generation. He has been stranded three times, first by the war itself, then by the hollowing-out of European society which followed the peace, and finally by the betrayal of the revolutionary ideals which had earlier promised to replace the failed and defeated empires of Germany and Russia. Like so many of his contemporaries, he is trapped in a repeating cycle, endlessly failing to remake his fractured past. The deeper meaning of extra-territoriality in Roth's work is not merely the loss of homeland but the total loss of the self which that homeland once expressed. The novel ends neither in tragedy nor triumph but in a pervasive emptiness. Franz Tunda, with his Teutonic Christian name and Slavic surname, personifies the impossibility of reconciling a failed past in Austria and an aimless future in pre-revolutionary Russia. Cast adrift from both, a displaced person in post-war Paris, like Roth himself he is an exile of the soul:

It was at this hour that my friend Tunda, thirty-two years of age, healthy and vigorous, a strong young man of diverse talents, stood on the Place de la Madeleine, in the centre of the capital of the world, without any idea what to do. He had no occupation, no desire, no hope, no ambition and not even any self-love. No one in the whole world was as superfluous as he.

That final adjective is revealing. The 'superfluous man' is a character type from the Russian fiction of the previous century, particularly the novels and short stories of Turgenev. He represents doomed Russian gentry, intelligent and sensitive enough to perceive his own lack of purpose but without the will to arrest it. He could be the writer Trigorin in

Chekhov's *Seagull*, who is 'good enough but not as good as Tolstoy'. He is kin to the characters in Maxim Gorky's two plays *Summerfolk* and *Enemies*, which explore the futility of an entire social class. When he describes Tunda as 'superfluous' Roth draws attention to his own Slav affinities. He writes in German but he is not really a German writer.

Roth addressed this issue directly in the mid-1920s after *Hotel Savoy* first appeared. He complained about its cool reception in Germany and Austria and compared it to the enthusiasm in Russia, where four separate Russian translations appeared shortly after its publication in the *Frankfurter Zeitung*. He even wrote a rather sour letter to a fellow journalist under the strap-line 'Am I a German writer?' It is a fair question. Do we trust the Austrian teller or the Slavic tale? *Hotel Savoy* and *Flight Without End* both look eastward towards the Russia which was only a few kilometres from his birthplace. In Brody and Lemberg, Roth would have heard Russian spoken in the streets and marketplaces. At the Rudolf Gymnasium he certainly read Dostoyevsky alongside Goethe and Schiller. When reviewing Murnau's *Der Letzte Mann* in 1925, the two writers he cited in comparison were Gogol and Chekhov. Eight of his full-length novels and two of his major collections of journalism contain scenes set in Russia. In his work, there are dozens of characters, major and minor, of Russian origin. One of Roth's great contributions to twentieth-century literature was to combine the two halves of his Galician inheritance. He stands with one foot on either side of the Austro-German/Russian border.

His dual identity is revealed most clearly in his next novel, *The Silent Prophet*, where the early years of the Russian Revolution are perceived from the standpoint of another extra-territorial. It was drafted in 1927 and 1928 and he offered it to the publishers Fischer Verlag shortly after his return from Soviet Russia. However, it was never completed and remained unpublished during his lifetime. Perhaps Roth was unable to reconcile the revolutionary narrative with his own residual scepticism. It certainly displays the same sense of betrayed ideals as its predecessors. Like the articles he wrote for the German press at the same time it warns of betrayal, just as *The Spider's Web* predicted proto-fascism six years earlier. Roth was one of the first journalists to visit the new Soviet republic and, many years before such writers as Koestler and Malraux, he identified the conflicts brewing within the communist leadership. In the mid 1920s, he hinted to friends that he was working on 'a Trotsky novel' and the central character bears a few superficial similarities to the founder of the Red Army. However, Friedrich Kargan has more in common with Gabriel Dan and Franz Tunda than any of the Bolshevik leaders. He is a border Slav with Austrian roots. Like Tunda, he is a stateless migrant with a German Christian name and a Slavic surname. In the opening chapters, Roth stresses his Habsburg origins and even adds some of his own fantasy biography, just as he had done with Tunda:

He was an unwanted, because illegitimate, child, the son of an Austrian piano teacher named Zimmer, to whom the rich tea merchant had refused his daughter. The piano teacher vanished from Russia, old Kargan had him sought for in vain after he learned of his daughter's pregnancy . . .

Kargan grows up at the western end of the Empire in Trieste and is apprenticed to a shipping agent, where his clients are 'deserters, emigrants and refugees crossing the Austrian border from Russia'. He masters several languages, including Russian, and is dispatched to one of Roth's characteristic Galician border towns to work with the local subcontractors who operate just within and occasionally well outside the law. Unsurprisingly, his colleagues are Jadlowker the Jewish innkeeper and the sleazy human-trafficker Kapturak. This time Roth gives the smuggler a detailed description and curriculum vitae. Kapturak is a small, spindly man with a sallow complexion and a profitable sideline as a quack doctor and a dodgy lawyer. He also has a lengthy criminal record and spends the winter months in prison polishing up his contacts with the police, emerging in the spring like a migrating bird to lead a new flock of refugees across the frontier. This section of the novel reveals that the trade in extra-territorials originated during the great pogroms of the 1880s. The post-war flood of refugees merely continued a process familiar for many generations. Some made landfall in New York's Ellis Island in the 1890s while others, including my own grandfather, arrived in London's Stepney and Whitechapel in the same fashion from similar *stetls*. They all had Kapturaks and Kargans somewhere in their pre-history.

Kargan begins his apprenticeship in 1908. This is a significant date; it was the moment when the Empire began to decompose into its competing national minorities. Roth transplants his crypto-Trotsky into his own extra-territorial Habsburg world. In borrowing again from his own autobiography, Roth is telling us that Kargan is not simply the agent of extra-territorials, he is their double. The novel is the next stage in Roth's journey through the spiritual geography of exile, and Kargan is a foot-soldier in the army of exiles who constantly populate his work. In the opening chapters he attends weekly meetings in the house of an expatriate Russian cobbler called Chaikin. His political education is conducted within a microcosm of displaced Eastern Europeans. These sessions are populated by the 'rebellious and dissatisfied', a multicultural and multinational assortment of 'adventurers and doubtful nationalities'. Here Roth draws heavily on his own journalistic impressions of migrants in *Journeys through Galicia*, published three years earlier. As in *Hotel Savoy* and *Flight Without End*, their clocks seem to have stopped. Their displacement is a product not of war or revolution but of the human condition itself. Roth compresses time almost cinematically, cutting and fading between fierce political debates among Kargan and his fellow agents provocateurs and detailed descriptions of the refugees' living conditions:

They ate in a cellar. They were given soup made of sausage scraps. A long table. Hurrying rattling spoons. Metal tableware. Noises of lips smacking, spoons scraping, throats gurgling . . .

This sense of suspended time persists after Kargan is arrested in the border tavern and transported as a political prisoner to Siberia. Here Roth reworks some of his reports and essays for the *Frankfurter Zeitung* – this time from his Russian travels in 1926. However, instead of developing Kargan's political education or sharpening his social awareness, much of his confinement is spent dreamily revisiting the sensations of his earlier years in Austria. He evokes the colours and textures of the towns of Central and Eastern Europe, the shape of a woman's shoes and the warmth of her skin. In his Siberian prison camp, his real exile is from his own identity. Franz Tunda and Friedrich Kargan are brothers under the skin and, just to emphasise the point, in an earlier chapter Roth makes a Hitchcock-like personal appearance: 'Had our lives not taken such differing courses, Friedrich would probably become my friend, as did Franz Tunda . . .'

As he emerges from behind the scenery Roth strips the documentary mask from the face of his own fiction. The closer we examine *The Silent Prophet* and all the other 'political' fiction of the 1920s, the more expressionistic and the less journalistic they appear. Not only does he conduct conversations with his own characters, he moves them from novel to novel, sometimes changing their roles and their locations and sometimes inventing new back-stories to propel the action forwards. Kapturak appears in five separate novels, smuggling Tunda, Kargan, Singer and Eibenschütz across the border, lending money to Trotta and changing currency for his cousin. He is not the only actor in Roth's repertory company recalled by popular demand. There is Kroy the coachman who appears under two different Christian names in the short stories 'Strawberries' and 'This Morning a Letter Arrived', and the coral dealer Nathan – or is it Nissen? – Piczenik (or possibly Pichenik) in *Tarabas* and *Leviathan*. When Roth is particularly pleased with a member of his ensemble, like Lieutenant Taittinger who has a bit part in *The Radetzky March*, he promotes him to Captain and casts him as the lead in *The Tale of the 1002nd Night*. When he requires a couple of servants in *The Capuchin Crypt*, he recalls Trotta's batman Onufrij from retirement and brings his father's old valet

Jacques back from the dead. As for little Mizzi Schinagl who makes her debut as a *süsse mädl* or girl of easy virtue in his first story 'The Honours Student', she returns to the cast list twenty years later in *The Tale of the 1002nd Night*, this time with her name above the credits.

As we know, Roth does much the same with his locations. His birthplace of Schwaby first appears as Shmerinka in *Flight Without End,* then as Zuchnow in *Job*, as Zlotogrod in *Weights and Measures* and *The Capuchin Crypt,* as Koropta in *Tarabas* and as Lopatiny in *The Bust of the Emperor*. The UFA film studios in Berlin would have been delighted with his economical scheduling and frugal use of resources.

All this cross-casting and sharing of locations is light years away from the documentary realism of the *Neue Sachlichkeit*. To twenty-first-century eyes it sometimes seems like an intertextual game, and there is something distinctly postmodern about the way Roth keeps asking the reader to verify his fictional falsehoods. However, he has a deeper purpose. In almost every novel, from the surreal *Hotel Savoy* to the impressionistic *Kaiser's Crypt,* he is reinventing a coherent Eastern Europe of the imagination.

More than that, by suspending time, by recalling characters and locations, he creates a totally personal world that is one half nightmare, one half redemptive dream. The nightmare is expressed through the never-ending war and the stream of stateless victims it trails in its wake. The dream is the pre-lapsarian Habsburg Empire where everything and everyone have their own space by the grace of the commander-in-chief. This is where Roth is almost alone among early twentieth-century Austro-German writers, even his friend Stefan Zweig. It is also where the two halves of his creative personality – the ironic and the romantic – underpin each other. For example, in *The Radetzky March* Franz Joseph is presented almost as a figure of fun, first when Carl Joseph's father secures a meeting with him in the Hofburg and then in his haunting interchange with the local rabbi while observing manoeuvres in Galicia. By making the Kaiser a tragi-comic figure Roth evades imperial nostalgia. In the same way he undermines Count Morstin's threnody for the old Empire by stressing the absurdity of his burial ceremony for the Kaiser's bust. On the other hand he constantly softens the documentary edge of his tales by peopling them with romantic archetypes. His borderlanders inhabit two worlds simultaneously – the harsh reality of post-war Galicia and a parallel fantasy world of Jewish tavern keepers and promiscuous gypsy girls straight out of the silent cinema.

Roth was not the only post-war writer in Mitteleuropa to benefit from his hybrid origins. The novelist Zweig and the poet Celan were also border Jews steeped in their multicultural heritage. However, Roth's fused influences – his early life on the eastern edge of empire, his first-hand experience of war, his brushes with modernism in Paris and Berlin, his observation of seismic political change in the Soviet Union and his bitter exile in the 1930s – combined to forge a unique literary voice.

His Jewish heritage was also important, although we should be careful not to mythologise it. Sidney Rosenfeld sees Roth primarily as a pilgrim in search of a lost father, fatherland and faith. He certainly carried all these burdens on his back throughout his short life. Yet he did so without special pleading. When he described himself as 'the last of the last of the Jews', it was in tones of self-mockery, not self-pity. He took a certain pleasure in being one of the *narunim* or fools of Brody. He liked to play the part of the traditional *batlan* described in *The Wandering Jews* – the itinerant jester who entertains at Hasidic weddings. *Batlanim* were not just comics. They also had the gift of prophecy, just like the *yurodivy* – the holy fools of Dostoyevsky and Pushkin. When his clear ironic gaze penetrates the surface of the world, Roth too is a *batlan* and like them he tells uncomfortable truths. From the prescience of *The Spider's Web* to the disillusion of *The Silent Prophet*, he stands on the edge of experience, observing and empathising but never committing. Like so many creative artists whose origins lay on the margins of the Habsburg world – particularly Jews – he earned the privilege of speaking truth to power.

Four

– Menuchim's Song –

T here is an apocryphal story that when the Habsburg Emperor Joseph II visited Brody in 1774 to relieve it of the burden of collecting taxes and proclaim it a *freistadt*, he conferred another honour on the town. Seeing the throng of black-clad Hasidim in the streets he exclaimed: 'This is my Jerusalem, so I can rightly call myself "King of Jerusalem", the title claimed by the kings of Austria.' From that moment until the town's privilege as a tax-free zone was withdrawn a hundred years later, the Kaiser's poetic epithet stuck to Brody like glue.

Another celebrated Ukrainian teller of tales, the Israeli S. Y. Agnon, set his novel *The Bridal Canopy* there and perpetuated its mythical status as the Galician Jerusalem. The combination of Jewish, Ruthenian and Habsburg culture which Roth encountered in the years before he began his studies in Vienna left a symbolic residue in almost everything he wrote. Jewish experience – their displacement, their need to have multiple identities and their marginal position in society – provided endless material for both his fiction and his reportage. Jewish life lies at the heart of *Job* and *Leviathan*. Jewish characters dominate *Hotel Savoy* and *Tarabas.* His most powerful collection of essays concerns itself entirely with *Ostjuden,* both in their Slavic homelands and in the ghettoes of Berlin, Vienna, Paris and New York's Lower East Side. The further he travelled from Galicia, the more Jewish values penetrated his prose. Even after his supposed conversion to Catholicism, they haunted his final tales. Above all they held up a mirror to the fractured world he continued to witness throughout his wanderings.

It is not surprising then that in the last few decades, Jewish commentators have claimed Joseph Roth as one of their own. Apart from the American scholar Sidney Rosenfeld, the celebrated playwright and screenwriter Sir Ronald Harwood has also made out a powerful case for Roth as primarily a Jewish novelist. We should be circumspect about this claim and not confuse the teller with his tales. When he wishes to, Roth can evoke *Yiddishkeit* with as much sensitivity as Agnon or Sholem Aleichem or Isaac Bashevis Singer, but he always remains at one remove from his subject matter. He was never a child of the *stetl.* He was an Austrian of Jewish extraction from a predominantly Polish region. Although he was born into a Jewish family and lived largely among Jews until his mid-twenties, even in his youth he stood outside Orthodox Jewish life. His mother tongue was not the Yiddish which was the lingua franca of Galician Jews but *hochdeutsch*

– the High German which his mother taught him as an infant and which was the teaching medium in his primary school. Maria Grübel Roth was an ambitious single parent from an educated family and she made sure that her son was enrolled in the Baron Hirsch Grundschule in Brody. Here he learned Polish and German and studied Goethe and Schiller alongside Hebrew and Jewish history. Bronsen tells us that he also read the Psalms and the prayers in the original but mainly in order to translate them into German. Roth's grandfather was a stonemason who lived close to the Brody Jewish cemetery and whose first language was almost certainly Yiddish. However, Roth's possessive mother brought her son up to be a German Jew – or more accurately, an Austro-German Jew – rather than a Galitzianer. When Bronsen interviewed family friends and relatives, many of them remarked that Maria always kept Joseph distant from his contemporaries, and described her accompanying him on his journey to school until well into his teens. Bronsen paints a picture of a family which was insecure socially and financially, living in genteel poverty and probably wishing to keep a distance between themselves and the *stetl-juden* who made up more than 60 per cent of Brody's population. Whatever the reason, this placed young Moses Joseph Roth half inside and half outside his Jewish origins – a position he occupied for the rest of his life.

It also fostered an ambivalent sense of his ethnic identity. In *The Wandering Jews*, he never once reveals his own Jewish origins. Even when he writes of the border *stetls* or of the Jewish district of the Josefstadt in Vienna, he scrupulously avoids the first person singular or plural. Nor does he sentimentalise the life of the little Jewish villages on the Russo-Polish-Austrian frontier. His landscape is harsh and his portraits severe. His most traditional Jewish character, the poor infant teacher Mendel Singer in *Job*, beats his sons, mistrusts his daughter and fails to empathise with his increasingly desperate wife. Like his biblical model Job, Singer's role in the novel is to suffer and to curse the uncomprehending deity. The society he portrays is far distant from the comfortable communities depicted in the tales of Sholem Aleichem. Until its redemptive ending, the only tenderness shown in the narrative comes from the Christian peasant carter Sameshkin, a drunken reprobate, who comforts Mendel on his journey to acquire the papers which will allow him to emigrate to America.

There is no special treatment in any of his fiction for the marginalised Galician *Ostjuden*. Rosenfeld suggests that Singer's serial disasters are somehow the product of his failure to live the simple pious life of his fellow Hasidim and his punishment for emigrating to the unfeeling modernity of the New World. This is certainly one reason for his guilt, first when he learns of his son's death in the war and then when he witnesses his wife dying of a broken heart and his daughter's mental disintegration. However, this is Mendel's perception of himself and not the author's. Throughout his work, Roth balances cultural sensitivity with cool objectivity.

The primary role of Jews in his fiction is to suffer. Almost all of his Jewish characters live in deep poverty. There are only two prosperous Jews in his entire output and their function is to highlight the gulf between their own good fortune and the fate of their compatriots. Bloomfield the expatriate American businessman in *Hotel Savoy* and Shemeriah in *Job* both offer redemption, but paradoxically they intensify the pain of those around them. Bloomfield (*né* Blumenfeld – another name-changer) returns to his Galician homeland but not to fulfil the hopes and dreams of his desperate fellow countrymen. He has come to the borderlands to visit his father's grave because 'home is above all where our dead lie'. In *Job,* Mendel Singer's oldest son also changes his name – from Shemeriah to Sam – and prospers when he settles in New York. He sends for his family to join him from Zuchnow and for a moment it seems as if the family's suffering might end. Yet when he dies as an American soldier in the Great War this actually precipitates the novel's catastrophic climax – encapsulated in his mother's death and his sister's schizophrenia. When redemption finally arrives it is in the shape of Singer's disabled and slow-witted third son, Menuchim, now rather improbably reborn as a musical genius. He brings salvation to his father not from the new world but from the old. He is now leading a group of players from Eastern Europe on a tour of the West and it is only when they reach the USA that father and son are reunited. For Rosenfeld this symbolises the superiority of ancient *stetl* values over the shallow modernity and materialism of Jewish New York. He sees Roth as an unresolved migrant *Ostjude* reaching back to his own Hasidic roots for reconciliation. But if we examine the final pages of *Job* closely we can see that there is another counterpoint running beneath the novel's principal melody and it provides a clue to the novel's symbolic structure.

It is no accident that Menuchim is a musician. Roth prepares us carefully for his re-entry into the story throughout the final third of the novel where the sound of music is heard on almost every page. When Mendel contemplates returning to his homeland to fetch his damaged child he sings and dances the Psalms like a good Hasid at the festival of the Rejoicing of the Law. In his Lower East Side garret he sings regularly 'on good days and bad ones . . . when he had thanks to offer to heaven and when he feared it'. When his wife Deborah hears of Sam's death, she sings 'in a deep male voice, as if there were another singer in the room'. In the blasphemous depths of his despair, as Mendel burns his prayer shawl, phylacteries and holy books, he 'calls a terrible song after them'. His therapy for his loss is to look after neighbours' children, and as he rocks their cradles he sings 'an old, old song': 'Say after me Menuchim: In the beginning God created the heaven and the earth . . .'

His one comfort is a phonograph on which he plays a collection of 'new songs from Europe'. But they are not new songs. The music which soothes his pain is *klezmer*, the wedding music of the Pale of Settlement which was born on the borders of Romania, Austria, Ruthenia and Russia during the eighteenth and nineteenth centuries. Its instruments are those of itinerant musicians – violin, clarinet and double bass – and its melodies borrow from the folksongs of every place of passage from Transylvania to Odessa, blended with the cantorial melisma which Roth would have heard every Saturday morning in Brody. One tune captivates Mendel: 'It ran like a little brook and murmured softly; it was vast as the ocean and roared. Now I am hearing the whole world, thought Mendel.' It is called 'Menuchim's Song' and it is the key which finally unlocks and releases Mendel's misery.

Why is music the metaphorical thread which binds the closing chapters of the novel? Why is Mendel's surname Singer? Roth gives us the answer in *The Wandering Jews*, when he remarks that unpronounceable Jewish names were a constant burden to their owners. A Russian name would become German in Vienna and would then be Anglicised in London. Often the name denoted a function in society – a Schneider was a tailor, a Handelsman was a trader, and so forth. I can add a brief personal note. My own father's cousin, born near Kiev, was called Muskant. He became an orchestral cellist in the UK. His brother was a band leader. Muskant is a contraction of the German/Yiddish word *musikant*. Perhaps Mendel's surname conjures up his spiritual origins both in the synagogue and under the bridal canopy? We hear no music in the Russian first half of *Job* but when Mendel is adrift as an alien in New York it becomes a recurring leitmotif. It may be fanciful to suggest that music cast a similar spell over Roth's subconscious but it is worth remembering that one of his Brody relatives was a cantor. Some of the most affecting pages in *The Wandering Jews* describe Yiddish music and the Yiddish theatres where it was often performed. Here is his description of it in the section which deals with the Jewish communities of Berlin:

I think I can best describe it as a mixture of Russia and Jerusalem, of popular song and psalm. It is music that blends the pathos of the synagogue with the naivety of folk song. The words when you hear them would seem to demand a light and jaunty melody. But when you hear the song, it's a sad tune, 'smiling through tears . . .'

Klezmer is wedding music and its fusion of smiles and tears is the aural equivalent of the wine glass which the couple smash when marital vows are exchanged. The shattered glass stands for all the contradictory elements in a wedding, from the broken hymen of the virgin bride to the mixture of joy and sadness with which the parents part with their daughter. Most of all it represents the omnipresence of misfortune and the human capacity to overcome it. He uses similar language a couple of pages earlier, where he presents Jewish customs and traditions as a metaphor for the instability of diaspora life. What binds these communities together is not faith but fatalism:

Those Jews observe the religious customs more out of pious habit than religious need; they think of God only when they need him, and given their luck, they need him fairly frequently . . .

There is nothing sentimental about this passage. It has the sour pragmatism of a stand-up comic in the Borscht Belt. When Roth writes of *stetl* life he makes no exceptions. If Jews have a tough time it is because they are an acute case of the sickness suffered by all of Europe's displaced peoples. As we know from *The Wandering Jews* they are 'always the third party and always lose'. Trawling through the cast lists of his fiction, it is often difficult to decide whether a character is Jewish or not. When Andreas Pum argues angrily with his Maker in *Rebellion* there are echoes of the milkman Tevye haranguing God in Sholem Aleichem's stories, but Roth never suggests that Pum is a Jew. He is merely a specific example of a general case. In *Hotel Savoy* and the *Neue Sachlichkeit* fiction of the 1920s, he often gives his protagonists Jewish characteristics and sometimes Jewish names but his primary concern is their destiny rather than their origins. He rarely attributes the fate of his characters to the fact that they are Jewish. Apart from his descriptions of burgeoning Nazism in *The Spider's Web* and a few passages in *The Radetzky March*, he hardly ever makes direct mention of anti-Semitism.

One might expect a book with the title *The Wandering Jews*, published in Germany during the rise of Hitler, to depict the hatred and suspicion of Jews which Roth must have witnessed on the streets of Berlin. What we see instead are the common indignities of migrant life perceived through Jewish eyes. He observes quarantine and border controls as they impact on all stateless persons rather than individual minorities. Consider his use of the first person plural in this passage:

We do not realise that our whole life has become a quarantine, and that all our countries have become barracks and concentration camps, admittedly with all the modern conveniences.

Who are 'we' in this sentence? Not immigrants, let alone *Ostjuden*. Roth the Galician expatriate with an Austrian passport is accepting responsibility for the way his temporary German home infringes the human rights of all migrants whatever their origin. It is the same when he writes about cards of identity. In the preface to the second edition of *The Wandering Jews*, published in 1937 when the Nuremberg Laws had already been passed, he turns from lamenting the specific fate of German Jews to a general condemnation of all the oppressive by-products of the nation state:

... a human life nowadays hangs from a passport as it once used to hang by the fabled thread. The scissors once wielded by the Fates have now come into the possession of consulates, embassies and plainclothesmen. No one loves victims, not even their fellow victims.

Of course, by this time direct reference to institutional anti-Semitism was dangerous, and indeed in 1932 a reference to Jews in his essay *Die Scholle* was actually suppressed by his Munich editors. However, like everything else in his writing, his presentation of Jewish experience is underpinned by paradox. While Roth the polemicist condemns their displacement Roth the journalist celebrates the vibrant culture which they import into the West. This fusion of opposites is particularly evident whenever he writes about Orthodox Jewish religion. What attracts him

to Galician *Yiddishkeit* is not faith but tradition –
what he calls their 'pious habit'. His description of
the festival of *Simchat Torah*, which marks the annual completion of the reading of the Pentateuch,
is a vivid example. He depicts the Hasidim, hand in
hand, swinging the Torah scrolls around like danc-
ing partners and kissing them with tears of joy. He is
moved by the eroticism of their dance and the way
in which it unites physical pleasure with spiritual
joy. His evocation of Yom Kippur is equally sen-
sual. Even though he is depicting the darkest day in
the Jewish year, it is another illustration of 'smiling
through tears'. On Kol Nidrei – the evening before
the festival when Orthodox Jews compute their sins
and prepare their vows of expiation – he describes
stillness so tangible that it is almost musical:

The great silence that deafens an otherwise almost orientally
noisy town oppresses even the lively children, whose shouting
and crying plays such a prominent part in the symphony of
the streets.

Roth was so pleased with this piece of descriptive
writing that he incorporated it almost verbatim into
the later work entitled *The Antichrist.*

There is one particular place where Roth is a
very Jewish writer indeed. His taste for paradox is
virtually Talmudic. The essence of the Talmud lies
in its rigorous questioning of every aspect of Juda-
ism – every belief, proscription and practice. It is

based on the dialectical method of 'either/or'. Every proposition in the Bible is placed beside its opposite and tested to destruction. We know that even in the enlightened Baron Hirsch school which he attended in his early years, Roth followed a traditional Jewish course of study. We also know that his grandfather was a devout Hasidic follower of the rabbi Baal Shem Tov. In the photographs of Brody from the early 1900s in the town museum, the streets are full of sallow kids with greasy side-locks, no doubt fresh from the local *yeshivot* – the tiny seminaries which are often located in private houses. You can see their modern equivalents in London's Stamford Hill or Crown Heights in Brooklyn, with the same curls and black skullcaps and fringed prayer garments peeping out from under their long black jackets. From the age of six they are divided into pairs and learn their religious faith by arguing violently with each other in heightened sing-song Yiddish. As they dispute, they rock backwards and forwards, exactly like the Hasidim depicted in *The Wandering Jews.*

Talmudic processes inform Mendel Singer's and Andreas Pum's arguments with God in *Job* and *Rebellion*. When God's ways defy logic, Roth becomes a temporary Talmudist and turns logic on its head. As in the biblical story of Job, he reframes God and makes Him mirror his own damaged creation. Similar paradoxes inform the plots of other tales, particularly when they involve the very devout or the very wicked. The narrative proceeds by contrary motion; the faithful are dragged down by their piety and the sinful are redeemed by their transgressions. Mendel Singer rises above his despair only after he burns his phylacteries and prayer books. He is a holy blasphemer. While *Job* is consciously constructed along the lines of a biblical parable the same ironies are evident in other stories less immediately concerned with issues of faith. The pogrom in *Tarabas*, when drunken Ruthenian soldiers smash up a Galician village, reaches its climax when a painting of the Virgin is revealed hidden beneath the plaster on a pub wall. Tarabas is a holy anti-Semite.

Talmudic paradox also creeps into such stories as *Rebellion* and *Confession of a Murderer*, both of which feature criminals as protagonists. Spiritual paradox pursues Roth to the end of his creative life. It is so central to his final completed novel that it informs even its title. *The Legend of the Holy Drinker* tells of yet another former murderer who achieves salvation as a destitute alcoholic under the bridges of the Seine.

Roth's relationship to Jewish belief is as counter-intuitive as the man himself. Some commentators have used the irritating phrase 'self-denying Jew' to describe his ambivalent relationship with his own *Ostjude* background. In the final chapter of *Understanding Joseph Roth* Sidney Rosenfeld writes:

. . . the evidence of his private letters and journal contributions show that he too was infected by the virus of German-Jewish self-hate, or a strain of it that might be better described as German-Jewish self denial, which, however, often found hostile expression when projected outwards.

It is an important distinction but it begs an equally important question. If Roth is in denial, what or who is the self that he is denying? At one level his fabricated autobiography, with its fantasy father and fictitious birthplace, denies his roots in the down-at-heel outskirts of Brody. This is convincing as amateur psychology but it is scarcely earth-shattering.

Roth is not the first writer to obscure his own origins. It might be more accurate to see his failure to acknowledge his own Jewishness in *The Wandering Jews* as a statement of journalistic integrity. In his foreword to the book he tries to identify his intended audience. He says that he is writing for those who 'might have something to learn from the East'. In other words, he hopes that they will be as open-minded as he is. In return he will be even-handed when he depicts the dark and light sides of Jewish culture.

Growing up on the margins of Austro-German civilisation, Roth was ideally placed to introduce his readers to a still neglected culture. As a Jewish Galitzianer he knew the *narunim* of Brody from the inside. By the same token he could also move almost invisibly from one segment of society to another.

With his Viennese higher education, his war service and his various postings as a foreign correspondent he could adopt the perspective of urbane cosmopolitans and working-class Austrian foot-soldiers. The photograph of him taken in 1926, wearing a rather elegant suit and sitting on a railway platform with a goods wagon in the background shows the Joseph Roth that he always wanted to be, poised between two worlds and observing both with equal clarity.

This is not the picture of a *stetl* Jew in self-denial. Rather, it is the portrait of a congenital non-joiner. This is a man who applies for an Austrian passport

and then lives in Berlin and Paris. This is an author who enjoys the life of a *flâneur* in 1920s Western Europe and then writes *feuilletons* pouring scorn on consumerism and the materialism of Weimar Germany. This is a penetrating film critic who spends three pages of newsprint celebrating the latest movie by Murnau and then satirises the vulgarity of contemporary cinema. More than anything this is *Muniu faktisch*, whose literary masterpiece *The Radetzky March* is marinated in nostalgia for the Empire destroyed a dozen years earlier and at the same time anatomises the self-delusion which destroyed it. How very Jewish. How characteristic of someone who was born astride two worlds and decided to remain extra-territorial for the rest of his life.

Roth was not compelled by poverty to live out of suitcases in hotels in the years before his Parisian exile. He was one of the most successful and best-paid journalists writing in the German language. If he was a wandering Jew, it was by choice. Even in Paris after the *Anschluss*, with his books banned and then burned, with his publishers closed down and his money draining away in the bars of the 7th arrondissement, he turned down invitations to emigrate to the USA. Was this because he still believed a miracle would restore the old Empire? In joining the circle which surrounded the Habsburg Crown Prince was he denying the reality of the post-imperial world? Or was he congenitally unable to belong anywhere?

Was he like the central character in *The Capuchin Crypt*, who concludes the novel with the words 'Where could I go now, I, a Trotta?' Once again, it is easy to play the amateur psychologist and see his displacement coming from his unresolved *Ostjude* identity. Yet it can as easily be constructed in cultural or political terms. Just as the multicultural Habsburg Empire provided an alternative to the nationalism which tore Europe apart at the end of the 1930s, so *Ostjude* values offered another equally positive model for a society without frontiers.

Of course there was one further option for Roth apart from emigration to the USA. Like many of his fellow German Jewish artists he could have settled in Israel. But true to form he turned his back on that escape route with equal resolve. Indeed, throughout his journalism of the 1920s and particularly in *The Wandering Jews*, he conducted an angry campaign against Zionism. He dismissed Theodor Herzl's putative Jewish state as vehemently as he rejected the nation states created after Versailles. In the opening section of the book he characterises Zionism as just another mutation of the nationalism which pulled the old empire apart. He reminds us that Eretz Yisroel was the invention of an Austrian journalist. He satirises the competing nationalist claims of Czechs, Magyars, Poles and Ruthenes before finally spinning off into his celebrated riff on how Jews are always the third party and always lose. These paragraphs are dismissive enough but they are nothing compared to what follows. A couple of pages later he discusses the expropriation of Palestinian land by early Jewish settlers:

The Arab's fear for his freedom is just as easy to understand as the Jew's genuine intention to play fair by his neighbour. And despite all that, the immigration of Young Jews into Palestine increasingly suggests a kind of Jewish Crusade because, unfortunately, they also shoot.

In the mid-1920s his use of the word 'crusade' is remarkable. It predates the Arab riots against the settlers by several years and it even anticipates the Palestinian response to the founding of the Jewish state. There is more to come. He reserves his deepest scorn for the idea of Jewish armies:

The European mark of Cain won't wash off. It is surely better to be a nation than to be maltreated by one. But it's a painful necessity all the same. Where's the pride for the Jew, who disarmed long ago, in proving once more that he is capable of squad drill!

This would be alarming if it had been published in the *Guardian* after the war in Lebanon in the 1980s or the invasion of Gaza in 2008. In 1927, when the democratic Weimar Republic government was hanging on to power by its fingernails and Hitler was waiting in the wings, it is totally prophetic, particularly from a writer who still thought of himself as Jewish. It is only when we reach the following paragraph that the underlying logic of Roth's argument becomes clear. In rejecting a Jewish state in Israel he is anything but a self-hating Jew. He is embracing the traditional values of the Jewish diaspora as practised in the eastern borderlands. For Roth *Ostjude* society and the multicultural Empire which sheltered it were symbiotic. To create a Jewish state was to deny Jewish history. In support, he cites the Galician Hasids who in the 1890s were already asserting that Israel was a blasphemy because it had been prophesied that Jews would only return to their homeland in the days of the Messiah. A century later Roth might have savoured the irony of the great-grandchildren of Galician *stetl* Jews now colonising the Mea Shearim district of Jerusalem, dressed like Polish Hasids, accepting Israeli passports but refusing to serve in the Israeli army and living under the protection of a nation whose very existence they denied. Roth's own rejection of Israel eighty years earlier was political not spiritual; it was grounded in history rather than faith:

Given all the millennial grief of the Jews, they still had one consolation: the fact that they didn't have such a fatherland. If there can ever be such a thing as a just history, surely the Jews will be given great credit for holding on to their common sense in not having a fatherland at a time when the whole world launched itself into patriotic madness.

Trust Joseph Roth to dismiss the Jewish state in the form of a very Jewish paradox.

There is one further savage irony which Roth did not live to witness. In a letter to his friend Stefan Zweig in 1935, he wrote that 'A Zionist is a National Socialist, a Nazi is a Zionist.' This is a shocking claim and some have put it down to his growing despair in exile and the effects of alcohol. However, it echoes passages in *The Wandering Jews* written eight years earlier when he was relatively healthy and success-ful. Describing the pious Hasids of Galicia, he says:

... this Jew is not a 'nationalist' in the Western sense. He is God's Jew. He does not fight for any Palestine. He detests the Zionist . . . His Jewish nation would be along the lines of a European state. The outcome might be a sovereign nation, but it wouldn't have any Jews in it . . .

In other words, for Roth the true Jew is diasporic. In 1927 when this was written, he could still imagine *stetl* values continuing into the foreseeable future. He had recently visited independent Poland and the young Soviet Union, and although he was worried about the prospects for the USSR he had witnessed surviving Jewish communities similar to his own Galician birthplace. He could see no reason why their robust Slavic diaspora should not survive for many generations.

When I visited Brody ten years ago, there was not a single surviving descendant of the communities

Roth met in the 1920s. Brody synagogue was a rain-streaked ruin and the Jewish cemetery was a crumbling wasteland of gap-toothed graves. Western Ukraine was second only to Poland in the numbers of its inhabitants transported to the death camps. At the time of my first journey to Galicia I was considering making a film about Roth and his 'flight without end'. I asked the distinguished journalist Neil Ascherson, himself of Polish extraction, if he would collaborate with me on the project. He replied that after the *Shoah* such a film would now be impossible. He was sadly correct. The Final Solution had comprehensively denuded Eastern Europe of Jewish life and culture. In a further irony, a portion of its few survivors were now settled in an Israeli state that during its conception had generated almost as many refugees and extra-territorials as Roth encountered in Austria, Germany and Russia in the 1920s. Today his vision of the life of 'the good Jew' is confined to the Brooklyn suburbs, the 4th arrondissement in Paris, Stamford Hill in London and the occupied territories of the West Bank. The lifestyle he celebrated in *The Wandering Jews* is only visible in the very places he despised.

What does this mean for the readership Roth was seeking when he wrote the preface to *The Wandering Jews* – 'the readers who feel they might have something to learn from the East'? It is a complex question. To begin with, Roth himself was a messenger, not a representative. He never lived the pious, deprived life of the *Ostjuden*. After his departure in 1913, he never revisited his birthplace. His own sufferings were self-inflicted, through exile, depression and drink, and he experienced them in Paris and not Brody. He was a creative writer and not a politician. His Galician model for community life is no more a prescription than his retrospective vision of the multicultural Empire. His dispatches from the borderland *stetls* offer a distillation of diaspora life not a prognosis. Even more, his fictional evocations of *stetl* communities are metaphors rather than documentary accounts. In asking his readers to learn from the East, he is suggesting that they absorb its values and spirit rather than re-create its social structure. In writing *The Wandering Jews*, Roth was continuing his lifelong search for an alternative to the nationalism which he saw poisoning the world in which he grew up. This is where his two main preoccupations – the vanished multicultural Empire and the lost world of borderland Jewry – join hands. His search for supra-nationality encompasses the whole legacy of his early years, from his identification with migrants to his mistrust of nationalism to his Talmudic love of paradox.

This gives us another reason why Roth demanded the right to be extra-territorial. He could no more acknowledge a State of Israel than he could accept being a citizen of Poland. Nevertheless he always maintained his respect for the rooted values of the communities which surrounded him in Brody. Just like Menuchim's song, which makes a redemptive journey from Zuchnow to East Houston Street, he transcended the *stetl*. His meditations on Jewish life are as contradictory and inconsistent as anything else in his work; they vacillate between tenderness, irony and anger according to his mood.

Yet there is one place in his writing – two thirds of the way through *The Radetzky March* – where he synthesises his two supra-national models, the imperial and the multicultural. Here he brings its two symbolic incarnations face to face. Shortly before the assassination of his heir in Sarajevo, Kaiser Franz Joseph decides to attend manoeuvres in the Galician district where Carl Joseph von Trotta is stationed. The old man's purpose is nostalgic rather than military. He simply wishes to revisit his early years as a young commander-in-chief. As he is shaved on the morning of his inspection, he recalls that as a Habsburg monarch his supreme rank is that of King of Jerusalem. He therefore has a duty to greet the local Jews. In a single sentence, Roth unites his own Jewish patrimony with the iconic roots of the Habsburg dynasty. When the Emperor meets his Jewish alter ego, the old rabbi holds up another crowned symbol – the scrolls of the Torah – and greets him with a prediction in the form of a Jewish prayer:

'Blessed art thou,' said the Jew to the Emperor. 'Thou shalt not witness the end of the world.'

At this moment the rabbi is both a prophet and a *batlan*. Roth knew that his readers would understand the irony of the rabbi blessing one of the culpable authors of the slaughter shortly to follow in the fields of Flanders and on the Russian frontier. The Emperor did not live to see the bloody end of his world. But his loyal and conflicted Galician subject Moses Joseph Roth did.

Five

– The End of the World –

On 8 January 1918, two years after Franz Joseph died, the American president Woodrow Wilson addressed a joint session of the US Congress. His ostensible task was to report on the progress of peace negotiations with Germany and her allies. His real purpose was to redraw the map of the world. The fourteen points which he presented to the assembly formed the basis of three treaties which dismembered three empires. At the gracious palaces of Versailles, Trianon and Saint Germain en Laye, Wilson, the French premier Clemenceau and Lloyd George met to refine the small print. (Three months after the October Revolution, Russia was otherwise engaged.)

In less than twelve months they created five new European nations and reduced Austria, Germany and Turkey to ghosts of their former selves. Huge chunks were sliced out of Germany and ceded to the new nations of Czechoslovakia and Poland, now reborn as a republic. Hungary was surgically separated from Austria and in the process Transylvania, Croatia and Moldavia were carved off to fatten up Romania, Czechoslovakia and the brand new old

Kingdom of the Serbs, Croats and Slovenes, which had not yet christened itself Yugoslavia. Several months later, while few were looking, Bukovina was transferred to Romania and most of Galicia handed over to Poland. The impact of these changes on Germany was so radical that it seems to have wiped away our memory of the simultaneous disappearance of the Habsburg Crown Lands. Joseph Roth on the other hand never forgot them.

When I made my first journey for the BBC through Eastern Europe in 1999, I interviewed the American historian Charles Ingrao. His description of the geo-political legacy of Versailles was a graphic metaphor for the vanishing trick which the allies performed on Mitteleuropa :

The twentieth century has been such a catastrophe because eliminating the Austro-Hungarian Empire was like a surgeon going in and taking out the stomach and liver and pancreas. You created a huge cavity.

One puzzling feature of this cavity is that it was almost invisible to spectators west of the Elbe. European literature groans under the weight of poetry and prose inspired by the battlefields of Northern France and Flanders. The English poets Wilfred Owen and Siegfried Sassoon, the American novelists John Dos Passos and Ernest Hemingway, and the German writers Eric Maria Remarque and Erich Kästner all produced legendary accounts of the slaughter of troops and civilians on the western front. Yet there were only two writers of genuine substance who concerned themselves with the impact of the Great War on the equally devastated eastern borderlands.

One was the fine journalist John Reed, who is best known for his vivid account of the Russian Revolution, *Ten Days that Shook the World.* Less familiar and equally vivid is his collection of impressions of the Russian front in 1915, published under the title *The War in Eastern Europe.* In Bukovina and Galicia, he witnessed the chaos and collateral damage which the Russian and Austrian armies trailed behind them when they advanced and retreated three times in less than a year. He attached himself to Russian units as they retook villages and towns already pulverised by the first wave of German and Austrian troops, and he described an ill-assorted Slavic army reinforced by conscripted Cossacks and Central Asian mercenaries stumbling across the Dniester and Prutt rivers towards the Polish frontier with the West. It is by far the best account of the Great War in Eastern Europe. His picture of Czernowitz, Tarnopol and Lemberg swamped by displaced prisoners and looting soldiery is only matched by the early novels of Joseph Roth, the one great writer to draw on the eastern campaign as an inspiration for fiction.

More than half of Roth's stories deal directly with the consequences of the war on the Russian frontier. Apart from their literary merit, they are important for several other reasons. They demonstrate how the consequences of the Great War infected the whole of the following decade and because they are fiction rather than journalism they reveal the after-effects of war on fully fleshed-out characters.

In his first, unfinished novel, *The Spider's Web*, the anti-hero Theodor Lohse drifts into fascism after he has been demobilised from the defeated German army. In *Hotel Savoy* Gabriel Dan and Zwonimir Pansin fetch up among the displaced migrants and refugees of a Slavic frontier town which could be Tarnopol or Lemberg three years after John Reed filed his dispatches from the battlefield. Franz Tunda begins his *Flight Without End* as he makes his way back from a Russian prison camp via Ukraine to Austria just as Reed did. Joseph Kargan's revolutionary career in *The Silent Prophet* only takes off after he has crossed the devastated landscapes of Galicia and Germany, where 'he had grown used to the idea of the sovereignty of certain death in Europe'. In *Rebellion* the hurdy-gurdy player Andreas Pum, a war hero who has lost a limb in the German retreat, carries the damage of the eastern front with him into a composite Berlin/Vienna of the early 1920s.

The legacy of war continues to influence the fiction of the 1930s. In *The Bust of the Emperor*, Count Morstin's world falls apart when he returns to his estate of Lopatyny after its incorporation into

Poland. At the turning point of *Fallmerayer the Stationmaster*, the protagonist exploits the fighting in Ukraine to escape to France with his Russian Countess. In Roth's penultimate novel *The Capuchin Crypt* Franz Joseph Trotta's world, like that of Dan, Tunda and Kargan, is terminally transformed when he returns from Russian imprisonment.

This sense of irreversible change is familiar to anyone who has read the *Neue Sachlichkeit* literature of Roth's German contemporaries. Ernst Toller, Alfred Döblin and Erich Kästner all examine the social and spiritual impact of war and political upheaval on the demobilised soldiers, rootless intellectuals, bankrupt businessmen and stateless refugees known in Austria and Germany as the *kriegsgeneration*. However, what is unique in Roth is the pervasive sense of personal loss. His war generation is not merely damaged by the violence of total war. They are deracinated and decultured and they have no reassuring homeland to fold them in its embrace. Even when he transports them to Vienna, Berlin or Zurich they are still haunted by flashbacks of the abandoned borderlands. From the edge of the world they witness the end of *their* world. What was once the frontier of a stable society has become, in Charles Ingrao's metaphor, a vacant cavity. This emptiness unites Roth's political fiction of the 1920s and the melancholy fables of his Parisian exile. It links people without a spiritual identity and countries without a political purpose.

This has tempted some commentators to see Roth's literary career as a descending curve from engagement into escapism. Rosenfeld, for example, divides his creative output into three phases, influenced respectively by the political turmoil of the 1920s, the trauma of the rise of fascism in the early 1930s, and the despair in exile prompted first by the electoral victory of Hitler and then by the *Anschluss*. Once again, this is only true as far as it goes.

In his early works Roth examines the various alternatives on offer in post-war Mitteleuropa and finds them all wanting. He dismisses fascism in *The Spider's Web*, revolutionary communism in *Flight Without End* and *The Silent Prophet*, and Weimar social democracy in *Right and Left* and *Zipper and his Father*. Here he shares something with his radical German contemporaries and he justifies the nickname he bestowed on himself in Frankfurt – *der Rote Joseph*, or 'Red Roth'. However his 'socialist' phase was restless and short-lived. As the Great War retreated into memory, he began to dig deeper into the distant past for his subject matter. In *Job*, The *Radetzky March*, *Weights and Measures* and *The Bust of the Emperor* a preoccupation with Europe's spiritual exhaustion was replaced by a growing obsession with the vanished cultures of the frontier *stetls* and the Empire itself. In *The Capuchin Crypt*, written on the eve of the *Anschluss,* he made one final effort to heave his own *kriegsgeneration* into the contemporary reality of rump Austria. When that ended in disillusion he took refuge in a kind of virtual reality. *The Tale of the 1002nd Night* is a bruised fairy tale set in the Austria of Johann Strauss waltzes, Dehmel confectionery, exotic foreign dignitaries and available *süsse mädeln.* Roth's personal political beliefs and his fiction followed the same path. By the time of his death in Paris four months before the outbreak of the Second World War he had buried Red Roth and embraced monarchism and Catholicism. His own endless flight had begun with an exploration of geography – the social landscape of Central Europe in the years after the Great War. Now it was ending by retreating into history – the burn-out of Habsburg Vienna in its final flush of creative energy.

That is one way of describing Roth's creative trajectory and it seems to satisfy many of his critics. However, it is not quite supported by the evidence. *The Tale of the 1002nd Night* was not a last escape into nostalgia. It was actually written *before The Capuchin Crypt.* Prompted by the shock of the *Anschluss*, Roth and his publisher decided to shelve *The Tale of the 1002nd Night* in favour of the darker, more controversial sequel to *The Radetzky March.* Concluding as it does with its hero adrift in a nation now fused with Nazi Germany, *The Capuchin Crypt* offered far greater contemporary relevance than the frivolous tale of Baron Taittinger and his girl of easy virtue Mizzi Schinagl in the Vienna of the 1880s. Roth's publisher, by the way, was now the Dutch firm of De Gemeenschaap. His German publisher Kiepenhauer had been closed down by the Nazis and all of his books were burned along with the works of his fellow 'decadent' German writers Mann, Zweig and Brecht. Published in Holland for a largely expatriate readership, *The Capuchin Crypt* was briefly safe from the fascist censors. Needless to say it too was soon suppressed in the Netherlands along with the rest of Roth's output when Hitler invaded the following year.

His final completed novel, the dreamy fable *The Legend of the Holy Drinker*, does seem to be a last attempt to escape into a more benevolent universe, but as it was published posthumously it is difficult to decide whether it was a new departure or a kind of literary therapy. Besides, chronology is never much help in deciphering Roth's artistic purpose, particularly in his alcohol-soaked, debt-laden final years. *The Capuchin Crypt* is flanked by a fairy tale and a fable in much the same way as *Job* was followed by the quasi-epic *The Radetzky March*. At the end of his life Roth continued along the same parallel and conflicting paths which he trod a decade earlier. One road led outwards to the damaged world of Eastern Europe between the wars and the other inwards to his own fragile soul.

To understand what linked these divergent strands and why his evocation of a vanished world is still relevant, it helps to return to his *seelenland-schaft* – his spiritual geography. That is exactly what Roth himself did in his final, flawed and fascinating exploration of that world, *The Capuchin Crypt.*

Once again, it is better to trust the tale rather than the teller. Roth himself called the novel a sequel to *The Radetzky March* and claimed that it portrayed 'the frightful death of the last corner of freedom in central Europe, the devouring of Austria by Prussia'. Both these statements are true as far as they go but *The Capuchin Crypt* has far more to offer than a mere tying up of the loose ends in the story of his homeland. In its own way it is as ambitious as *The Radetzky March.* It depicts the end of the world not once but twice – first in retrospect and again in terrible prospect. Roth had prophesied the *Anschluss* in the early 1920s but by the time it arrived he was too ill and too depressed to react with anything other than blank despair. It is left to readers to add their own postscript to the Trotta family saga. The German takeover of Austria only forms a grim epilogue in the final few pages of *The Capuchin Crypt.* The bulk of the novel is concerned with a restless and haunted scouring of what one of its characters describes as 'Austria's essence . . . not to be central but peripheral'. Like the coda to Mahler's 6th Symphony, another Austrian masterpiece haunted by catastrophe, it revisits all his main preoccupations and grinds them to dust.

Roth puts down a marker in the first four words

of the book: 'Our name is Trotta.' Like his first completed novel, *Hotel Savoy*, and unlike anything else, he wrote it in the first person. There is not even an unreliable narrator like the fictitious Joseph Roth of *Flight Without End* or *The Silent Prophet.* Then he chooses to make this first-person narrator announce himself in the plural. Like *The Radetzky March*, this will be the chronicle of a dynasty and this time it will be recorded from within – 'Trotta is *our* name.' Finally, even though 95 per cent of the story takes place in the past, it begins in the present tense. In other words, this will not be a retreat into history but an examination of how the past continues to poison the present. In particular, the after-effects of the Great War are still so potent that by the very end of the novel the protagonist has become a kind of zombie, a representative of the living dead:

To be obsolete among the living means something like being extra-territorial. I was extra-territorial among the living.

The choice of adjective is chilling; even more so because 'extra-territorial' can also be a noun and Trotta wears it as a badge of identity. Roth has returned one final time to the theme which has dominated his entire output. *The Capuchin Crypt* is a huge meditation on inner and outer displacement. As he revisits all the landmarks of his life and work, he argues that when it lost touch with its periphery, Austria abandoned 'its essence' – the multicultural equilibrium which underpinned its whole purpose.

The historical and geographical scale of the novel is even greater than *The Radetzky March*. At the very opening we are reminded of the 'hero of Solferino' who was ennobled by accidentally saving the Emperor's life. We are briefly reintroduced to the rural Slovenian backwater of Sipolje where the Trottas originated and to Vienna during the economic boom which followed the *Ausgleich* with Hungary. There are even passing references to America, where the nephew of the hero of Solferino has made his pile at the turn of the twentieth century. This narrative is delivered at one remove from the past. The narrator is now Franz Joseph Trotta, the cousin of Carl Joseph, the protagonist of *The Radetzky March*. As Roth had killed off Carl Joseph in the battle of Krasne Busk at the end of the earlier novel he needed to invent a new central character for its sequel. However, he had other more interesting reasons for shifting forwards in time and sideways in space. In *The Radetzky March* Carl Joseph Trotta grows up in Vienna and Moravia and visits the more distant eastern Crown Lands almost by chance after his expulsion from the cavalry, when he joins an infantry regiment stationed at the remote edge of the Empire. His cousin Franz Joseph is much more intimately connected with the Slav periphery. He speaks Slovenian and has regular visits from his

Slovene relative Joseph Branco, who also has friends and family in Galicia. Roth prepares us for this shift of focus to the Crown Lands on the novel's second page when Franz describes his father as dreaming 'of a Slav monarchy under the rule of the Habsburgs . . . a joint monarchy of Austrians, Hungarians and Slavs . . .' He is both 'a rebel and a patriot – a species which only existed under the Old Monarchy'. Unlike Carl, who has spent his entire youth trying to escape from his destiny as the Viennese scion of an ennobled family, Franz has been brought up as a 'Slav of the Empire'.

To emphasise the Slavic aspect of the novel, Roth immediately introduces two further recurring characters – a more distant cousin from Slovenia called Joseph Branco and his friend, the Galician Jewish coachman Manes Reisiger. In their company Roth transports us to the Galician front in the Great War and to Siberian exile. The long digression which follows, describing the captivity of Trotta and his two friends, is a reworking of similar passages in *Flight Without End*. It is only one of many echoes of his previous stories. Roth places a grave reflection on Austria's peripheral identity in the mouth of the Polish Count Chojnicki just as he did in *The Radetzky March*. This time it develops into a passionate plea for the retention of the imperial dependencies: 'The body politic of Austria is nourished and constantly replenished from the Crown Lands.'

There are many repetitions of earlier descriptions of provincial Austria-Hungary. When Franz visits the Galician *stetl* of Zlotogrod (another location revived from earlier tales) he observes its similarities with Sipolje – the K and K railway station, the uniform of the stationmaster, the blonde cashier – just as Count Morstin does on his tour of duty in *The Bust of the Emperor*. The cashier, whose double Franz has seen in 'Agram, Olmütz, Brünn and Keckemet', has become almost mythological. She is a 'latter-day Goddess of Depravity'. We pay a visit to Jadlowker's frontier tavern from *The Silent Prophet* and *Job* where refugees 'travel between a known past and a highly uncertain future'.

Yet everything is subtly but pointedly transformed. The cashier has been 'given her notice by history, and short notice at that'. The tavern where 'general confusion once prevailed' is 'eerily quiet', and Kapturak the smuggler is a 'silent shadow of his former self'. Roth has transposed his earlier melodies into a remote and discordant key. He adds a suspended cadence just to reinforce his message:

Only much later, long after the Great War which is now in my opinion rightly called the World War, because as a result of it we each lost a world, our own world, was I to realise that even landscapes, fields, nations, races, huts and coffee houses are bound to submit to the perfectly natural dominion of a powerful force with the ability to bring near what is remote . . .

When he uses the words 'in my opinion', who is speaking? Is it Franz Joseph Trotta, the displaced descendant of a minor Slovene officer, or Moses Joseph Roth, the displaced author who is no longer 'Red Roth?' Some critics have seen this passage as proof that in his works of exile Roth was escaping from the modern world into an alternative and very conservative reality. Rosenfeld attributes his embrace of monarchism in the early 1930s to his guilt at betraying his *Ostjude* roots as well as his alcoholism and his depression:

Beset by misfortune and homeless as never before, the despairing Roth now turned to the past and in his crowning work, *The Radetzky March*, he resurrected Old Austria in order that he might mourn its passing.

No one would deny that *The Radetzky March* is Roth's crowning work, but it was written immediately after the publication of *Job* when, despite his wife's mental illness and his decision to abandon Austria, he was reasonably comfortable in his own skin. His involvement with the circle surrounding the Habsburg heir and his adoption of the Catholic faith came several years later. Nor is it any more accurate to describe *The Capuchin Crypt* as a threnody for the old Empire. It is as paradoxical as anything else in his work. Roth identifies the paradox a few lines after Franz Joseph Trotta's reflections on the Great War, when he 'speaks of the misunderstood and also misused power of the old Monarchy'. The narrator (whether Roth or Trotta) never denies that Austria was the author of its own disintegration. However, by juxtaposing the words 'misused' and 'misunderstood' he suggests that dismantling the Empire was also a terminal failure of perception on the part of the West. When he says later in the novel that the Crown Lands were exploited to support their careless imperial capital he also implies that this 'misuse' was capable of remedy. In his eyes, the treaties of Versailles, Trianon and Saint Germain led to something far more abusive. They enshrined nationalism as the guiding principle of the modern world. Once again Roth places his attack on the nation state in the mouth of the Polish Count Chojnicki:

'I'm no patriot but I love my fellow countrymen. A whole land, a Fatherland, is something abstract. But someone from the same part of the world is something concrete.'

Chojnicki's role in the novel is made even more disorientating by a strange narrative device. In *The Radetzky March*, among the disputatious Hungarian and Czech officers, he is the single rational voice. In *The Capuchin Crypt* Roth splits him in two. For the first two thirds of the novel we assume that this is the same character who bade farewell to Carl Joseph in 1914 as he left for the front and his appointment with an enemy's bullet. It is only when his cousin

Franz Joseph has returned to a Vienna now shrunk and humbled by defeat that we learn that Chojnicki is actually the brother of the character in *The Radetzky March*. Carl Joseph's friend Xandl is now confined to the Steinhof mental hospital, where he spends his days with a ball of wool and two needles 'knitting the Monarchy'. His brother explains that 'as a private person he is as mad as a hatter, but where politics is concerned he is second to none.' He then gives us an example of the Count's political judgement, which is as close to the opinions of Joseph Roth as makes no difference:

'Austria is neither a state, a home nor a nation. It is a religion. The church and the idiot clericals who now rule us are trying to make a so-called nation of us. Of *us*, who are a supra-nation, the only supra-nation which has ever existed in this world.'

By 1938 Roth was too sceptical an observer of that world to believe that the misunderstanding of the Empire and its misuse of its dependencies could ever be reconciled. The new reality ordained by Woodrow Wilson and brought into being by Hitler and Horty and Mussolini would not allow it. Just as he examined, tested and rejected all the political systems on offer in *The Spider's Web*, *Right and Left* and *The Silent Prophet*, so in *The Capuchin Crypt* he walks away from the modernist seductions of interwar Vienna. The abstract aesthetic of Adolf Loos, the bisexual values of the Weimar intelligentsia, the chilly anger of the *Neue Sachlichkeit* and the worship of progress in the reborn industries of the new German Reich all wither under his blistering gaze.

Yet when he chronicles the end of his world it is not with anger but with a deep sense of loss. Count Xandl Chojnicki is one of two resonant symbols in the closing pages of the novel evoking a past beyond recall. Like the Empire itself, his description of the Crown Lands is both visionary and deranged. It is worth noting in passing that the Steinhof asylum where he is housed was the creation of the Emperor himself. Franz Joseph commissioned the great Secession architect Otto Wagner to design the hospital and decorate it with ravishing *jugendstijl* wrought ironwork and stained glass. Anyone able to recall the old Empire might remember that even psychiatric patients benefited from the final flowering of Habsburg culture. The second symbol is more intimate. When Trotta returns to Vienna, his wife has deserted him for a lesbian ménage with a fashionable interior designer. Without wife, without employment and purpose, he moves back into the family home and is reunited with his ageing mother. As their fortunes decline in the inflation of the 1920s, their comfortable bourgeois house is turned into a *pension.* His equally impoverished contemporaries move in as paying (or more frequently non-paying) guests. The one possession from their earlier life which remains is his mother's old piano. Yet since his return from the war the piano has been soundless. His mother explains that when he left for the war a mental aberration prompted her to have all the strings removed so that she would not be able to play. It is only years later when she misunderstands an enquiry after an old friend that Trotta realises she has become profoundly deaf. She had the strings taken away when she began to fear that she would no longer know whether she was playing correctly. It is another musical metaphor. Just as Menuchim's song in *Job* symbolised an old world redeeming the new, so Frau Trotta's silent piano seems to stand for the suppression of Austria itself.

The music her son asks her to play is not by Schubert or Mozart or Beethoven but by Chopin – a Slav. This may be a coincidence but if so it is a happy one. It accords with the redemptive role that the Slav lands play throughout Roth's work. It might also be a buried memory of another Slavic artist much admired by Roth. In Chekhov's *Three Sisters,* Masha's locked piano stands for her dysfunctional marriage. In the same way, the music that is missing from the Trotta household represents the peripheral world now severed from the Germanicised Austrian republic. Throughout *The Capuchin Crypt*, whenever Roth wishes to embody loss he turns to the east. While Franz Joseph Trotta recalls his first visit to Zlotogrod with the Jewish coachman Reisiger, the narrative flashes forwards to its destruction during the frontier campaign of 1915. Roth also places Trotta, Reisiger and Branco in the vanguard at the battle of Krasne-Busk, a turning point in the eastern campaign. This is also where Carl Joseph met his death in *The Radetzky March*. After the three friends are taken prisoner and deported to Siberia, they are protected by another survivor from an earlier novel, the Polish fur trader Baranovicz who swapped identities with Franz Tunda in *Flight Without End*. Earlier in the novel when Count Chojnicki rejects 'this crazy Europe of nation states' it is the 'Slovenes, the Poles and Galicians from Ruthenia, the kaftan clad Jews from Boryslaw' whom he sets up figuratively in opposition to the German world he calls the 'Nibelungen fantasy'. He also includes 'the horse traders from the Bacska' and 'the Moslems from Sarajevo', who are certainly not Slavs but are not Germans either. He also rejects the idea that Habsburg history was forged on the medieval Alpine banks of the Rhine: 'Austria is not to be found in the Alps, where you can find edelweiss, chamois and gentians but never a trace of the double eagle.'

If Roth is reinventing Austria in *The Capuchin Crypt* in order to mourn it, it is the centrifugal empire in which he grew up which he mourns and not the imperial palaces of Vienna's Hofburg, particularly now they are under the sway of the Berlin Reichstag. In the final two pages of the novel Roth introduces one last and rather desperate symbol for the mutability of Old Austria – the hound which follows the narrator from his regular café to the last resting place of the Emperor. The Jewish café proprietor has packed up for the night and will shortly, if he is lucky, abandon an Austria now under Nazi rule. The old waiter has also been given his cards. Only a dog remains and it is made to carry a heavy metaphorical load on its back. Like the narrator it is called Franz; it is a German shepherd and it shadows the hero on his last journey to the Capuchin Crypt. Roth shows the resting place of the Habsburg dynasty being invaded by a German interloper. The weight of the *Anschluss* has become so oppressive that it crowds out all the other rich memories planted in the novel's earlier chapters. There is no space left in Roth's migrant soul for his beloved multicultural construct. The teller can no longer believe in his own tale.

Yet the novel is much more than merely a requiem for a departed society. In particular, the chapters devoted to Sipolje and Zlotogrod and the rhetoric of Count Chojnicki in either of his two incarnations propose an alternative reality which outlived the author and the Thousand Year Reich that drove him to an early grave.

My own search for Joseph Roth and his spiritual geography began in the palaces and cafés of imperial Vienna. The film which I made there thirty years ago was a celebration of the city in the first decade of the twentieth century when, in the words of my friend and collaborator Michael Frayn, 'the Empire was going out with the brilliance of a star burning itself up'. It was pure chance which drew my attention away from the intellectual glitter of Klimt and Kraus and Freud and Wittgenstein to their Galician contemporary.

Even Roth himself was susceptible to that glitter. He was seduced by it just as Carl Joseph von Trotta is when he visits the capital with his ageing mistress and witnesses the Corpus Christi procession. Roth returned to Vienna's high season in *The Tale of the 1002nd Night* at the same time as he was reading its last rites in *The Capuchin Crypt*. Seventy years later both halves of his Habsburg paradox are still with us. The philosophy and the visual art, the architecture and the music of Secession Vienna have all left their fingerprints on our own post-imperial world. So too has Austria's centrifugal periphery, although it took half a century to reassert its claims on our attention.

I chose to follow Roth to the edge of the former Crown Lands only after three empires – Habsburg, Nazi and Soviet – had been consigned to the catafalque of history. Even then in the 1990s the nationalism hated by Count Morstin and the extra-territorial Franz Joseph Trotta still made one last-ditch attempt to impose itself on the borderlands, not least in the western half of Ukraine where Roth was born. The

Orange Revolution which dragged the country away from Russian hegemony was born in the baroque squares of Lviv. As I write, the two visions which Roth explored – centripetal and centrifugal, nationalist and multicultural – are still engaged in a tug of war. Ukraine has yet to decide between its residual nationalism and its symbiosis with the Slavic continent to the east.

It is here that Roth's reputation survives the sometimes patronising judgement of his critics. His early fiction still holds up because it reframes our perception of the Great War and its consequences. It foresees not only the rise of totalitarianism in Germany but also its mirror image in Russia. It even imagines the worst excesses of nationalism persisting beyond the defeat of both systems. When he draws back from the political turmoil of 1920s Mitteleuropa and returns to the final Habsburg years which preceded it, it is not in nostalgic retreat but in quizzical exploration. Other writers have given us sensitive depictions of *stetl* life – the Yiddish teller of tales Isaac Bashevis Singer and the more acerbic Israeli S. Y. Agnon. However, neither of them relates Orthodox Jewish culture to the world which surrounded it as perceptively as Roth does in *Job*. As for his undisputed masterpiece *The Radetzky March*, my own and many other readers' entry point to his imaginative landscape, it may not have the philosophical weight of Musil but it presents the contradictions of European society on the eve of the First World War with a humanity and social reach unmatched by any other writer. If the fables and parables which he wrote in exile during the 1930s seem slight by comparison, each in its own way adds to his unique legacy as the laureate of displacement. The various threads he spins in *Tarabas*, *Weights and Measures*, *Fallmerayer the Stationmaster* and even *Confessions of a Murderer* are woven together in *The Capuchin Crypt* into a tapestry of the extra-territorial 1930s which still has lessons to teach us about Bosnia, Romania, Ukraine and all the other debatable lands left in limbo after what that premature prophet Francis Fukuyama termed 'the end of history'.

History no more ended in 1989 than it did after the Kaiser's death in1916. It continued exactly as before and in much the same places. Joseph Roth would not have been surprised to see virulent nationalism returning to Sarajevo just when the rest of the world had forgotten it. One cannot imagine him ignoring the edges of Europe just because they had slipped off the front pages of the newspapers. His abiding gift and his greatest curse was to be devoutly counter-intuitive. What could be more perverse than to apply for Austrian citizenship when Austria was on its knees and his native Galicia was being absorbed into a reborn Polish Republic? Even in the midst of inflation and political murder it was better to be supra-national than live under a mutant species of nationalism. When Austria followed the same path, he continued his restless pursuit of paradox in the Weimar Republic and Soviet Russia. The greatest irony of his life was the way in which his very despair, like that of Franz Joseph Trotta, opened his eyes to the darkness around him:

I saw myself, as I had for so long since my return from the war, as someone who was wrongly alive. I had, after all, accustomed myself for a long time to observing all the events which were described in the newspapers as 'historic' with the judicious eye of someone who no longer belonged to this world! I had for a long time been on indefinite leave from death. And death could interrupt my leave at any second. What did things of this world matter to me?

But they did matter and they matter to this day. They may have taken a terrible toll on Roth the man but they left Roth the writer prophetic to the very end.

– Selected Works by Joseph Roth –

available in English translation

The Spider's Web (trans. John Hoare; Granta)
Hotel Savoy (trans. John Hoare; Chatto & Windus)
Rebellion (trans. Michael Hofmann; Granta)
The Wandering Jews (trans. Michael Hofmann; Granta)
Flight Without End (trans. David Le Vay; Peter Owen)
Zipper and His Father (trans. John Hoare; Granta)
Right and Left (trans. Michael Hofmann; Granta)
The Silent Prophet (trans. David Le Vay; Peter Owen)
Job (trans. Dorothy Thomson; Granta)
The Radetzky March (trans. Michael Hofmann; Granta)
Tarabas (trans. Winifred Katzin; Granta)
The Bust of the Emperor (trans. John Hoare;
    Chatto & Windus)
Confession of a Murderer (trans. D. I. Vesey; Granta)
Weights and Measures (trans. David Le Vay; Peter Owen)
The Emperor's Tomb (*The Capuchin Crypt*)
    (trans. John Hoare; Granta)
The Legend of the Holy Drinker (trans. Michael Hofmann;
    Granta)
The String of Pearls (*The Tale of the 1002nd Night*)
    (trans. Michael Hofmann; Granta)
What I Saw: Reports from Berlin (trans. Michael Hofmann;
    Granta)
Collected Shorter Fiction of Joseph Roth (trans. Michael
    Hofmann; Granta)
Joseph Roth: A Life in Letters (trans. Michael Hofmann; W.
    H. Norton & Company)
The Hotel Years (trans. Michael Hofmann; New Directions)

nh

Notting Hill Editions

Notting Hill Editions is devoted to the best in essay writing. Our authors, living and dead, cover a broad range of non-fiction, but all display the virtues of brevity, soul and wit.

Our commitment to reinvigorating the essay as a literary form extends to our website, where we host the wonderful Essay Library, a home for the world's most important and enjoyable essays, including the facility to search, save your favourites and add your comments and suggestions.

To discover more, please visit
www.nottinghilleditions.com

Other titles from Notting Hill Editions*

Journey to Armenia
by Osip Mandelstam

Osip Mandelstam (1891–1938) was a Russian poet and essayist.
He visited Armenia in 1930 and during the eight months of his
stay he rediscovered his poetic voice and was inspired to write
an experimental meditation on the country. This edition includes
the companion piece *Conversation about Dante*.

'*Journey to Armenia* takes its place among the outstanding
masterpieces of twentieth century literature.' – Bruce Chatwin

Questions of Travel: William Morris in Iceland
by Lavinia Greenlaw

The great Victorian William Morris was fascinated by Iceland,
which inspired him to write one of the masterpieces of travel
literature. The poet Lavinia Greenlaw follows in his footsteps,
combining excerpts from his Icelandic writings with her own
response to the country.

'At a time of endless half-truths and moral shilly-shallying,
Morris's eccentric integrity shines out.'
– Fiona MacCarthy, *The Guardian*

The Foreigner: Two Essays on Exile
by Richard Sennett

Sennett explores displacement through two vibrant historical
moments: mid-19th-century Paris, with its community of
political exiles, and the Jewish Ghetto of Renaissance Venice,
where state-imposed restrictions on outsider groups had
surprising cultural connections.

CLASSIC COLLECTION

The Classic Collection brings together the finest essayists of the past, introduced by contemporary writers.

Drawn from Life – Selected Essays of Michel de Montaigne
Introduced by Tim Parks

Grumbling at Large – Selected Essays of J. B. Priestley
Introduced by Valerie Grove

Beautiful and Impossible Things
– Selected Essays of Oscar Wilde
Introduced by Gyles Brandreth

Words of Fire – Selected Essays of Ahad Ha'am
Introduced by Brian Klug

Essays on the Self – Selected Essays of Virginia Woolf
Introduced by Joanna Kavenna

All That is Worth Remembering
– Selected Essays of William Hazlitt
Introduced by Duncan Wu

*All NHE titles are available in the UK, and some titles are available in the rest of the world. For more information, please visit www.nottinghilleditions.com.

A selection of our titles are distributed in the US and Canada by New York Review Books. For more information on available titles, please visit www.nyrb.com.